"The One Page Business Plan
does something outrageous!
It causes very busy people
to stop and think.
As they start to write...
it confirms both their clarity
and their confusion!"

— Jim Horan
President
The One Page Business Plan Company

WARNING – DISCLAIMER

This book was designed to provide information in regard to the subject matter covered. It is not the purpose of this manual to reprint all of the information available to the author/publisher, but to complement, amplify and supplement other sources.

Use of The One Page Business Plan® does not in any way guarantee the success of an idea or organization, nor does it ensure that financing will be made available. When legal or expert assistance is required, the services of a competent professional should be sought.

The author/publisher shall have neither liability nor responsibility to any person or entity with respect to any loss or damage caused, or alleged to be caused, directly or indirectly by the information contained in this book.

If you do not wish to be bound by the above, you may return this book to the publisher for a full refund.

Published by:

The One Page Business Plan Company
1798 Fifth Street
Berkeley, CA 94710
Phone: (510) 705-8400
Fax: (510) 705-8403
www.onepagebusinessplan.com

ISBN 10: 1-891315-02-1
ISBN 13: 978-1-891315-02-2

Book Design by: Melodie Leidich
Cover design by: Jim McCraigh
Edited by: Rebecca Salome
Proofed by: Lynne McDonald
Printed in the United States of America

The One Page Business Plan®

*The Fastest, Easiest Way
to Write a Business Plan!*

By Jim Horan

Non-Profit Edition

We Have a Rich History with Non-Profits

Non-profit organizations have been successfully writing One Page Business Plans since 1994. Food banks, youth programs, foundations, hospitals, churches, schools, cities and associations all eagerly embraced our first book, *The One Page Business Plan for the Creative Entrepreneur*. Thousands of non-profits have written and implemented effective One Page Plans with this simple and effective planning methodology.

But as time went on, we wanted to do more. We wanted to keep non-profits from having to wade through the business-speak of entrepreneurs, business owners and corporate executives. We wanted a book with the language of non-profits for non-profits. We wanted a book that was filled with specific tips, techniques, templates and sample plans exclusively for non-profits... all designed to make writing a One Page Business Plan faster and easier.

And so this book, *The One Page Business Plan for Non-Profit Organizations*, was created just for you! Like others before you, it will help you live up to your promises to boards, management, staff, volunteers and clients by clearly defining your organization's direction... all in concise, easy to communicate and actionable terms.

Academy for Entrepreneurial Leadership, Univ. of Illinios
Alameda Alliance for Health
Allies in Recovery
Alzheimer's Care Clinic
American Baptist Homes of the West
American Conservatory Theatre, Seattle
American Medical Association
Assoc. for Self-Employment Success
Association of Unity Churches
Bay Area Entrepreneur Association
Bay Area Independent Publisher's Association
Bay Area Regional Technology
Bay Area Social Services
Big Brothers Big Sisters Santa Clara
Burlingame Library Foundation
CA MEP
CA Micro-enterprise
Caring People Alliance
Catholic Charities
Center for Attitudinal Healing
Center for Community Benefit Organizations
Center for Holistic Therapy
Center for Human Services
Center on Juvenile & Criminal Justice, San Francisco
Central Coast YMCA
Charles Cole Memorial Hospital
Chesapeake Innovation Center
Children's Hospital & Research Center Oakland
City of Oakland - CEDA
Community Cons School District 15
Connecticut Jr. College
Costa Rica TLA
Dental Services Group
Dominican University of CA
Downtown Burlingame Business Improvement District
East-West Healing Arts Center
Foundation for Integrative Oncology
Fremont Unity
Global Family
Home Educators Association of VA
Hopeworks
Hutchinson Unified School District

Illinois Coalition Against Domestic Violence
Institute for Management Consultants
Jewish Vocational Center, SF
John Muir Mt Diablo Medical System
Jr. Achievement - Capetown
Jr. Achievement - Fudan Univ.
Jr. Achievement - Hong Kong Univ
Jr. Achievement - East China Univ.
Jr. Achievement - Jiaotong Univ.
Jr. Achievement - Shanghai U.
Jr. Achievement - Tsinghua U.
Jr. Achievement - Witwatersrand
Jr. Achievement International

Since 1994 over 5,000 Non-Profits have used the One Page Business Plan®

Just Say Yes
Juvenile Diabetes Foundation
Kaiser Permanente
Kidsteem
LaSalle University Institute for Non-Profit Management
Lesbian Gay Bisexual Transgender Youth Program, San Francisco
Lombard Elementary Sch. Dist. 44
Louisiana Association of Non Profits
Louisiana Foundation for Entrepreneurship
Meals on Wheels
Med Camps of Louisiana
Mobile County Public School System
Muckleshoot Tribal Health Clinic
NECC – Local Outreach Ministry
Never too Late
No. American Riding for the Handicapped Association
Norfolk Baptist Association
North Penn School District
Northern Illinois Food Bank
Novato Youth Center

NV MEP
Oakland Children's Hospital
Oklahoma Jazz Hall of Fame
Our House: A Home & A Haven
Pacific Center
Palo Alto Unity
People Assets
Phoenix Children's Hospital
Profit-4-Kids
Profits to Kids Charities
Providence Services Medical Center
Renaissance Pleasure Faire
Ritter House
Rotary International SBA
Safe Blood Africa Project
San Antonio Community Hospital
San Francisco Interfaith Council
San Francisco Shakespeare Festival
Scripps Health Foundation
Seafood Producer's Cooperative
Second Harvest Food Bank of the Inland Northwest
Shea Therapeutic Equestrian Center
So. Oregon Child & Family Council
Stamford Health System
Tamarino Leadership Project
The Soul of America Project
The Vision For Tomorrow Foundation
The Well Project Company
The Wellspring
The Whittier Institute
Truth at Work
United for Courage
Unity in Marin
Unity of Jacksonville
University of British Columbia
University of Pennsylvania Center for Education Leadership
USC Orange County Bus. Forum
Valley Presbyterian Church
Villanova University, Dining Services
Volunteer Center of NW Chicago
Walnut Creek Community School
Walnut Creek Unity
Washington Manufacturing Services
Westmoreland Health System
Womens Initiative for Self Employment
YEO - Orange County
YMCA Hawaii
YMCA of the Upper Main Line

Foreword

What Others Are Saying

The One Page Business Plan takes a complex process and makes it simple!

We must run our organization like a well-run business, or we do not get to serve all of the children we want to serve! The One Page Business Plan has helped us align our Board, management team, paid staff and volunteers! We are now truly focused on what is important... helping kids!

Gary L. Montrezza, Executive Director, Big Brothers Big Sisters of Santa Clara County

The One Page Business Plan has been a tremendous tool for our 300+ member spiritual community. This process brought our spiritual community clarity about our vision, enhanced the Board and Ministry Leadership's ability to articulate the vision to others, helped our individual ministrys' awareness of how their plan relates to the community plan...and has helped us have quicker recoveries from breakdowns because as a community we now have a common focus and purpose.

Reverend Richard Mantei, Unity In Marin

Our One Page Plan has helped turn some 'social justice good-hearted souls' into better organized managers.

H. Dennis Smith, Executive Director/CEO, Northern Illinois Food Bank

Our One Page Plan saved our agency! We were in deep financial trouble, our accountants had lost control of our books and our government contracts were not paying on time. We created a very clear, concise plan using The One Page Business Plan that resulted in discipline and structure that got us back on track!

Dan Macallair, Executive Director, Center on Juvenile & Criminal Justice, San Francisco, CA

I've never seen a better way to deploy an organization's purpose and plans than with this brilliant, simple, straightforward approach to planning.

Frank Tiedemann, CEO, Children's Hospital & Research Center Oakland

Jim Horan is a master at creating a model and simplifying a vocabulary for those in the nonprofit and social venture and entrepreneurship professions that captures the competitive dynamics of our time. Boards, executives, and managers are all pressed for time. Plans need to be simple, clear and actionable! One Page Plans are just that!

Peter H. Hackbert, Ph.D., Academy for Entrepreneurial Leadership, University of Illinois

Non profits need to operate more like for-profit businesses.   Too often NGOs put off business planning due to staff capacity and difficulty in identifying measurable objectives. The One Page Business Plan for Non-Profits more clearly links objectives to mission with a method that is straightforward, takes less staff time and gets people working on the right things!

Lyn Ciocca McCaleb, Board Chair, The Coral Reef Alliance

With very tight budgets, even small mistakes can spell disaster for a fledgling non-profit. I knew I needed a road map to minimize costly missteps, but did not have the time or resources to develop an exhaustive strategic plan. The One Page Plan is simple and straightforward; I used it to carefully and thoughtfully launch my non-profit. To date my plan has proven its worth multiple times over!   The One Page Business Plan is an exceedingly valuable tool for any non-profit.

Tracy O. Tamura, Executive Director, Kidsteem™

"You must
simplify.
You must make
the complex simple,
then you must
make it work."

— I.M. Pei
Master Architect

Author's Note

If you are responsible for the leadership and operations of a non-profit, you must have a clear plan!

Then you must communicate it, execute it, and deliver the results. That is your responsibility and your promise!

The hungry, poor, needy, homeless, sick, elderly, immobile, blind, amongst many others, are counting on you and your organization to deliver the services you promise!

For those of us who are concerned about the air we breathe, the water we drink, the damage being done to the oceans, lakes, rivers, rainforest and countless other environmental tragedies... we are counting on you and your organization to deliver on your promises.

Your grant makers, donors, volunteers, in-kind contributors and supporters are counting on you to be extraordinarily efficient and effective in the delivery of your services. When you took their time, money and support... you made a promise!

Being effective and efficient in the service of others is no easy task! Especially when you do not have all the resources it takes to do the job the way you know it should be done... and probably never will. But that is the role and responsibility of the leadership in the world of social entrepreneurship.

To accomplish your mission, you must have a well thought-out plan, executed superbly. Everyone in your organization must literally be on the same page.

I encourage you to be mindful and disciplined about the choice of words in your plan(s)... your words count! Do not rush the process... most One Page Business Plans do not get powerful until about the third or fourth draft. There is a lot riding on your words, so make each one count.

This book was created to be in service of you and your entire team. I hope the tools and techniques in this book help you to bring a new level of focus and clarity to your important work. The One Page Business Plan is a process, a tool that has been used successfully by over five thousand non-profit and not-for-profit organizations... I think it can work for you.

If we are successful in helping you, please let us know. If you have suggestions, we would love to hear them. Need help, we have hundreds of consultants around the country that are in service of non-profits.

Jim Horan
Author, Consultant, Speaker

How to Use This Book and CD

The primary purpose of this book is to help you get your plan onto paper. It has been carefully crafted to capture the plan that is in your head.

Carry this book with you, write in it, use it as a container for capturing your thoughts as they occur. If you have multiple non-profits, partners or managers, have them get their own copy.

It's not necessary to do all the exercises in this book. If you can write your One Page Business Plan by reviewing the samples — skip the exercises. They are there to help guide you through the process if you need help.

This book does not look like the typical business planning book — it isn't intended to. The exercises and examples are meant to stimulate you. The graphics and images are meant to guide you. If they look playful, be playful and explore. If they look analytical, be analytical and focused. The examples and samples are from real non-profits. They are meant to show you how powerful a few words or a well-constructed phrase can be.

Do not underestimate the power of the questions that appear simple! They are simple by design. If you do not get an "aha" from them, have somebody ask you the questions. Important insights may begin to flow.

This book is divided into ten sections with the focus on the five elements of The One Page Business Plan. You can start anywhere. It's OK to jump around!

There are many different ways to use and interact with this book. Exercises can be done:

• by oneself

• with a planning partner (another Executive Director)

• as a management team

• as a group (multiple Executive Directors, your Board, other professionals)

• with a paid advisor

 The Non-Profit Tool Kit CD at the back of the book contains The One Page Business Plan Templates, bonus exercises, One Page Budget Worksheet, plus One Page Scorecards for monitoring and tracking your results.

VISION
MISSION
OBJECTIVES
STRATEGIES
ACTION PLANS

Table of Contents

VISION
MISSION
OBJECTIVES
STRATEGIES
ACTION PLANS

Introduction

The One Page Business Plan® for Non-Profits

*"Planning is a process...
not an event!*

*One Page Plans
are living,
changing,
evolving
documents!"*

The concept of The One Page Business Plan® was conceived in the fall of 1994 to help entrepreneurs and small business owners create simple, concise business plans. It did not take long before I found myself working with social entrepreneurs and executive directors of non-profit organizations.

I learned that many of the same issues entrepreneurs were struggling with, builders and leaders in non-profits were struggling with also. Executive directors needed to have a plan for their agency, but did not have the time to write one. They needed a plan because their Board demanded they have one. Funders and grant makers insisted that they needed to know where the organization was going beyond the programs they had been funding. Executive directors needed a compelling plan to be able to attract new Board members, key executives, talented employees and committed volunteers.

Executive directors also consistently commented to me that although their organization was committed to solving important social problems... they needed to run their organization with some of the mind set, and some of the tools of business. They knew that their organization needed the discipline, structure, clarity, and accountability that a business plan would bring to them. And yet, most of the executive directors I met either had a business plan that was less than satisfactory by their admission, or had attempted to write a business plan and just gave up.

Without a doubt, some of the absolute best One Page Plans I have seen in the last twelve years have been written by executive directors. Why? Executive directors are extremely passionate about the cause or issue their organization is trying to solve. They also are always searching for money and people... they have to be great communicators. They talk to a tremendous number of people and have to be effective in their communications. They must make their case in the most compelling manner possible, as quickly as possible. People have short attention spans.

Executive directors love The One Page Business Plan. It helps them communicate their story, their plan, quickly and effectively. I hope this book helps you create focus, alignment and better results in your non-profit. The world needs what you are doing.

Our Observations...

Why One Page?

You are busy, your time is limited. The people that need to understand your non-profit and plan are busy. They (you) are action and results oriented. Most of us are not good at prose writing... it takes too long to write a well-written sentence, paragraph, page or chapter. And far too long to read. People need to be able to read a plan in about five minutes. They want the essence... the key points. Then they want to talk... to ask clarifying questions, come to agreement... and then take action.

Why Plan?

Some need to write plans to get funding for their non-profit. Most people write plans because they either want or need to achieve different or better results. Plans are blueprints; they describe what is going to be built, how it will be done, and by whom... and the results to be measured.

Why Written Plans?

The spoken word is too fluid; we have a tendency to ramble; when we speak we almost never say it exactly the same way... frequently we forget to share some of the most important details... or spend too much time on the unimportant things. When we write, we choose our words more carefully. Writing takes time, usually much more time than talk. The written word requires a higher level of mindfulness and attention to detail. The written word also produces a contract with yourself and others that can be reread, refined... a source for reflection and mindful change if necessary.

Asking people simple questions... works!

People love to talk about their passion, causes... and solutions! They can easily answer questions like, what are you building, what will your organization look like in three years, what has made your non-profit successful to date, what are the critical structural projects and programs you have underway or planned, what do you measure to know if you are on track... and of course, why does your non-profit exist.

The Power is in 5 Key Questions!

Business plan terminology is problematic. Depending on where you went to school, and the companies/organizations you have worked for... the terms Vision, Mission, Objectives, Strategies and Plans probably mean something different to you than the person sitting next to you. We have learned business planning "definitions" just don't work. We have refined our questions over ten years with thousands of business owners. The five questions we will teach you are simple, easy to remember and are equally appropriate for the non-profit executive director, board member, volunteer or staff member.

About Planning Processes

Starting with a blank page wastes valuable time!

The examples and the fill-in-the-blank prompts are learning aids... designed to help you learn and master the One Page Business Plan technique quickly. We have learned that most people learn by seeing examples, so we give you lots of examples.

The dreaded "writers block" can easily be eliminated by the use of our proprietary fill-in-the-blank templates. Our templates make the creation of any portion of your business plan easy. Use the fill-in-the-blank templates to quickly capture your thoughts and create the first draft. You will also find that the extensive list of templates can spark your thinking and make sure that you are thinking about your "total" business.

Your managers and professionals can and should write One Page Business Plans!

The number one issue executives share with us is that they need their people to work on the right things... and achieve specific results! There is a simple solution: have your managers, program directors, paid staff and volunteer leaders create One Page Business Plans for their departments, projects or programs. This methodology works equally well for departments, projects and programs... and this workbook contains examples and templates to help create them.

Final Thought: Plans are important... Execution is critical!

Executives invest in planning because they want and need results. Plans are valuable because they provide the blueprint for where you are taking your organization and how you will get there... but ultimately the plans are only as good as the execution. Establish processes like the scorecard tracking and monthly progress and performance reviews to monitor the implementation of your plans.

What is a One Page Business Plan?

The One Page Business Plan is an innovative approach to business planning that captures the essence of any organization, project or program on a single page using key words and short phrases.

Most companies use the process to create not only the company's overall plan, but to create a plan for each supporting department, project and program. Since the creation of The One Page Business Plan in 1994, thousands of non-profits have successfully used the process to bring structure, alignment and accountability to their organizations.

The flexible methodology makes it possible for all managers and teams in the organization to each have a plan. The standard format makes it easy to review, compare and understand plans.

One Page Business Plans work because:
- Plans actually get documented
- Plans are understandable
- Plans are easy to write, easy to update
- Every manager or team has one

The process creates:
- Alignment
- Accountability
- Results

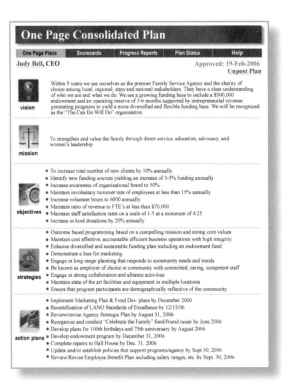

And Many Ways to Use It

Annual Planning Process

- Complete plan for small non-profits
- Executive summary for large organizations
- Project & program plan development
- Plans for support & administrative functions
- Professional & leadership development
- Framework for compensation systems
- Solid basis for developing budgets

External Presentations

- Fund development
- Volunteer recruitment
- Strategic alliance development
- Strategic hires
- Executive summary for bank/other funders
- Advocacy

Research and Development

- Initial draft for new programs
- Framework for potential expansion
- Proforma for mergers & acquisition
- "What if" for downsizing & restructuring

Process and Performance Management

- Clear structure for measuring outcomes
- Benchmark to measure progress against priorities
- Improve cross-functional communications
- Creates culture of accountability & responsibility

Business Plan Terminology is Confusing

There are no universally acceptable definitions for the terms Vision, Mission, Objectives, Strategies or Plans. How you use these terms depends entirely on what school you went to and what companies and organizations you have worked for. Many companies never successfully complete their business plans because they cannot agree on the basic terminology. We solved the problem!

We translated the five standard business plan elements into five simple and universal questions:

Vision: What are you building?

Mission: Why does this non-profit exist?

Objectives: What results will you measure?

Strategies: How will you build this non-profit?

Plans: What is the work to be done?

Writing a business plan for a department or program?

Modify the Mission and Strategy questions by replacing the word "non-profit" with department or program:

Department Usage	Program Usage
Mission: Why does this department exist?	Mission: Why does this program exist?
Strategy: How will you build this department?	Strategy: How will you build this program?

Business Plans Can be Simple and Clean

The Best Way to Understand The One Page Business Plan is to Read One... One Page Business Plans can generally be read in about five minutes or less.

Alzheimer's Care Clinic
FY2006 Business Plan Summary

vision

Within the next three years grow the Tri-County Alzheimer's Care Clinic into the primary resource for quality community-based services for the elderly needing Alzheimer care.

mission

Provide supportive services for the elderly and their families that maximize independence and dignity.

objectives

- Provide services to 350 individuals who have Alzheimer's or a related dementia.
- Provide case management services to 180 individuals in Tri-County area.
- Provide Ombudsman services in Tri-County; 4,800 contacts with residents.
- Operate the Tri-County Adult Day Support Center at 35 average daily census.
- Operate the Metro Adult Day Support Center at 26 average daily census.
- Serve 110,000 meals through the Meals on Wheels Program.
- Serve 1,000 seniors through the OMI Senior Center.
- Increase fee-for-service revenue to $525,000; 25% above last year.
- Obtain additional $125,000 in Foundation funding

strategies

- Develop and execute a marketing plan that effectively increases revenue from fees.
- Renew contracts with Madison and Perkins counties at 5% increased funding.
- Provide motivation and support to Program Directors to increase performance.
- Obtain greater support from foundations and other donors.
- Develop a knowledge management process for internal and external best practices.

action plans

- Create a marketing plan by Jan. 31st and implement immediately.
- Develop proposals for County contracts by Feb. 15th.
- Submit 3 new proposals to 9 Tri-County Foundations by May 31st.
- Develop and implement a staff motivation plan by Aug. 31st, includes bonus & prof. dev.
- Meet with key funders at least once every 6 months; first meeting Sept. 20th.

The Power and Magic
of Writing

"Writing allows others to participate in your dream and give you feedback."

There is magic in the written word! Especially when they're your words about an idea that you have been thinking and talking about for sometime. Somehow the process of writing initiates the transformation from idea to reality. It also does many other wonderful things.

Things get clearer when you write. Of course at first the process can feel very awkward, and the results seem poor and anything but clear. But given time and patience, the process results in a connection of the mind with the reality of the paper. Thoughts begin to develop into images. Images turn into key words and short phrases. An outline begins to emerge, and the clarity builds.

If you stick with your writing, you also get focused. In the beginning, you'll have many ideas, more than you can ever implement. But the process of capturing them on paper results in a conscious and unconscious ranking and prioritization. I believe it is important to capture as many of your thoughts regarding your products, services and programs as possible without critiquing them. The natural process of writing will keep the best and strongest of your ideas. Your vision and mission will become more concise through this evolutionary process, resulting in a focused approach.

Writing allows others to participate in your dream and give you feedback. Writing provides a consistent forum, whereas in conversation the context changes each time you speak. Allowing others to participate and help support your idea to its next step is crucial to your overall success. The Lone Ranger mentality is no longer necessary nor effective.

The written word also produces a contract with yourself that results in immediate action. Haven't you found that if you make up a grocery list and leave it at home you almost always remember everything on the list? Many users of The One Page Business Plan® report that as soon as they begin to write their action items — some of which they have been thinking about for years — they start to take action on them. *I think it's magic!*

Writing takes time, usually much more time than talk. The written word requires a certain level of artfulness and thoughtfulness in expression. In writing, we do not ramble on and on, as we do in speech. We choose our words more carefully. The words remain to be reread, refined, a source for reflection and mindful change if necessary."

—Thomas Moore
Care of the Soul and Soulmates

Why The One Page Business Plan Works

"Business Plans don't have to be complex and cumbersome.

The One Page Business Plan is meant to be simple and to help you get focused quickly."

Simplicity

The One Page Business Plan® is effective because it takes a complex subject and makes it simple. It's easy to read and understand. If you are the writer, you will know when you are finished because you have effectively covered all of the important elements of your business plan.

Focus

The One Page Business Plan® works because it focuses on what's important. There is no room for fluff or filler. The use of key words and short phrases tells your reader that only the essence is being presented for review. The fact that this business plan is only one page communicates that the investment in reading is limited.

Versatility

The One Page Business Plan® works because it's a tool for communication. If you are an Executive Director, this one page document can be an important tool for communicating to existing or prospective board members, employees, partners, volunteers, donors, funders or banker the kind of non-profit you are building and how you plan to build it.

Consistency

It's an effective communication tool because you send the same message to every person you give it to — unlike the spoken word, which may change every time you speak. Additionally, with the written word, you have chosen your words carefully and you are communicating only the most important elements of your business plan.

Readily Understandable

The five elements of the One Page Business Plan® are readily understandable. As you read each section, the business plan element telegraphs the kind of information being presented. You know the Vision Statement is going to be expansive and idealistic. You expect the Mission Statement to be powerful and customer oriented. Objectives should be realistic and measurable. Strategies are well thought out, and Plans are action oriented.

Flexibility

The One Page Business Plan® works because it's easy to change and update with your latest thinking. An important thought in the morning can be in your plan that afternoon. Capturing those "moments of clarity" quickly and in a useful manner will preserve them for further review, consideration, and possible action.

So what's the benefit of having a one page plan? It's your plan, your ideas, in your words. It's a reference point for any significant business or financial decision you may be considering. It's simple, concise, and it's you. The people that have the ability to help you can have a complete overview of your non-profit at a glance. Attach your budget and you're ready for a meaningful discussion.

Business Plan Myths

- All business plans are in writing.

- They must be long to be good.

- Their primary purpose is to obtain financing.

- It's easier for others to write business plans.

- You can and should do it by yourself.

- It takes six months, a significant amount of executive and staff's time, and expensive consultants.

- If completed, it will sit unused on a bookshelf.

- My non-profit is too small; business plans are for much bigger organizations.

- I know where I am taking my organization; I do not need a written business plan.

- I can just pay for a consultant to write the plan for me, that will be good enough.

Let's dispel the myths...

VISION
MISSION
OBJECTIVES
STRATEGIES
ACTION PLANS

Assessments
What's Working? What's Not?

"Too many people over plan and under execute.

Plan for what is critical… then execute the plan."

Intuitively you know the status of your organization… but when is the last time you stopped and gave it a checkup? Took a real look under the hood?

This section has three 10 Point Assessments to help you quickly determine what is working in your organization, and what isn't. We've also included a 10 Point Personal Assessment for you to do a little personal checkup, if you so desire.

These assessments are designed to help you to quickly take the pulse of your non-profit organization, which areas are strong, which aspects need attention. As with all of the exercises in this book, they are meant to be done quickly, relying on your intuition, state of mind and frankly, what is keeping you up at night and/or making you smile.

We encourage you not to overwork these assessments. In our workshops we give participants about five minutes to do the overall organizational assessment on page 26.

It's possible that not all of the categories on the 10 Point Assessments will apply to your non-profit, if so, you have two choices, 1) ignore those that do not apply; 2) modify the category to reflect an area of your organization that is critical to your success.

Want to include your Board or management team in the process? Make a copy of the assessment, and have each member rate the organization… and then share the results. Discuss why you agree, and disagree!

If you have an established non-profit you should find the Financial Health and Performance Management Process assessments helpful. If you don't understand all the categories or business processes listed, ask members on your Board with financial and business process expertise to explain them to you… these are critical processes that you and your team will want to master.

As you work through your plan, be sure to come back to these assessments to ensure your plan addresses the key issues you identify here.

What's Working in Your Non-Profit? What's Not?

Step 1: Rate each of these areas on a scale of 1 to 10; 1 = disaster 10 = brilliantly successful.

Step 2: Reflect on why you scored each element the way you did. Circle one or more of the reasons that influenced the rating. (FTI = Failure to Implement, ½❤ = half heartily executed plan, External = external forces, i.e. economy)

	Significance Rating	
1. Service Volume or Activity		1 2 3 4 5 6 7 8 9 10 FTI ½❤ People Process Time $$ External
2. Service/Program Quality		1 2 3 4 5 6 7 8 9 10 FTI ½❤ People Process Time $$ External
3. Overall Financial Health, Controls & Processes		1 2 3 4 5 6 7 8 9 10 FTI ½❤ People Process Time $$ External
4. Marketing/Community Outreach		1 2 3 4 5 6 7 8 9 10 FTI ½❤ People Process Time $$ External
5. Board of Directors & Outside Advisors		1 2 3 4 5 6 7 8 9 10 FTI ½❤ People Process Time $$ External
6. Management Team & Staff		1 2 3 4 5 6 7 8 9 10 FTI ½❤ People Process Time $$ External
7. Volunteers		1 2 3 4 5 6 7 8 9 10 FTI ½❤ People Process Time $$ External
8. Strategic Partnerships & Collaboration		1 2 3 4 5 6 7 8 9 10 FTI ½❤ People Process Time $$ External
9. Internal Administrative Processes		1 2 3 4 5 6 7 8 9 10 FTI ½❤ People Process Time $$ External
10. Performance Outcomes/ROI		1 2 3 4 5 6 7 8 9 10 FTI ½❤ People Process Time $$ External
Overall Assessment		**1 2 3 4 5 6 7 8 9 10**

Step 3: Make a check mark in the Significance Rating box for 3 – 4 elements you must dramatically improve in the next 6 – 12 months. It is highly doubtful you can make all of them 10's in the next year.

Where are the Opportunities for Improvement?

In left column: Identify key projects or areas that influenced your assessment.
In right column: Quickly brainstorm actions that can be taken to improve execution/performance.

Key Projects	Action to Improve or Maintain

| **Example for Service Volume:**
New Student Enrollment Program takes too long, too complex, all manual | Create simplified web-based application, auto checking for missing fields, user & staff tracking capability |

What is the Financial Health of your Non-Profit?

Step 1: Rate each of these elements on a scale of 1 to 10; 1 = disaster, 10 = brilliantly successful
Step 2: On page 29 identify the key elements/issues that influenced your rating.
Step 3: On page 29 make note of what needs to be changed to correct the problem areas.

1. Cash & Cash Reserves	N/A 1 2 3 4 5 6 7 8 9 10
2. Credit Line Usage/Availability	N/A 1 2 3 4 5 6 7 8 9 10
3. Revenue from Retail/Profit Centers	N/A 1 2 3 4 5 6 7 8 9 10
4. Fundraising/Capital Campaigns	N/A 1 2 3 4 5 6 7 8 9 10
5. Unrestricted vs. Restricted funds	N/A 1 2 3 4 5 6 7 8 9 10
6. Expense Control & Cost Containment	N/A 1 2 3 4 5 6 7 8 9 10
7. Accounts Receivable & Bad Debt	N/A 1 2 3 4 5 6 7 8 9 10
8. Accounts Payable & Other Current Liabilities	N/A 1 2 3 4 5 6 7 8 9 10
9. Loans & Long-Term Debt	N/A 1 2 3 4 5 6 7 8 9 10
10. Accounting Systems & Controls	N/A 1 2 3 4 5 6 7 8 9 10
Overall Assessment	**1 2 3 4 5 6 7 8 9 10**

Step 4: As you develop your plan, be sure to come back to this page to address the issues identified here.

Where are the Opportunities for Improvement?

In left column: Identify key issues that influenced your assessment.
In right column: Brainstorm actions that can be taken to improve low ratings or maintain high ratings.

Problem Areas or Successes	Action to Improve or Maintain
Example for Fundraising: Collection of pledges too haphazard.	Offer monthly credit card option, encourage payment in full, use computer tracking to streamline

Planning & Controls: What's Working?

Step 1: Rate each of these management processes; 1 = disaster, 10 = brilliantly successful
Step 2: On page 31 identify the key elements/issues that influenced your rating.
Step 3: On page 31 make note of what needs to be changed to correct the problem areas.

1. Planning: Annual & Multi Year Processes   N/A 1 2 3 4 5 6 7 8 9 10

2. Budget Process   N/A 1 2 3 4 5 6 7 8 9 10

3. Financial Statements   N/A 1 2 3 4 5 6 7 8 9 10

4. Monthly Business Reviews   N/A 1 2 3 4 5 6 7 8 9 10

5. Forecasting/Projections   N/A 1 2 3 4 5 6 7 8 9 10

6. Post Audits (projects & programs)   N/A 1 2 3 4 5 6 7 8 9 10

7. Project & Program Controls   N/A 1 2 3 4 5 6 7 8 9 10

8. Signature Authorization Controls
   for Expenditures   N/A 1 2 3 4 5 6 7 8 9 10

9. Department Level Plans & Budgets   N/A 1 2 3 4 5 6 7 8 9 10

10. Compensation & Incentive Systems   N/A 1 2 3 4 5 6 7 8 9 10

Overall Assessment   **1 2 3 4 5 6 7 8 9 10**

Step 4: As you develop your plan, be sure to come back to this page to address the issues identified here.

Where are the Opportunities for Improvement?

In left column: Identify key areas that influenced your assessment.
In right column: Brainstorm actions that can be taken to improve low ratings or maintain high ratings.

Problem Areas or Successes	Action to Improve or Maintain
Example for Post Audit: Outside auditor notes fundraising expenses are not in line with money raised.	Develop very specific goals & budget to reflect best non-profit practices.

How are you? A Personal Assessment (optional)

Step 1: Rate each of these aspects of your life; 1 = disaster, 10 = great, could not get any better
Step 2: On page 33 identify the key elements/issues that influenced your rating.
Step 3: On page 33 make note of your first impressions on what you would like to change.

1. Physically	1 2 3 4 5 6 7 8 9 10
2. Mentally	1 2 3 4 5 6 7 8 9 10
3. Relationships at Work	1 2 3 4 5 6 7 8 9 10
4. Your Role at Work	1 2 3 4 5 6 7 8 9 10
5. Personal Finances	1 2 3 4 5 6 7 8 9 10
6. Life Outside of Work	1 2 3 4 5 6 7 8 9 10
7. Sense of Community	1 2 3 4 5 6 7 8 9 10
8. Plans for Retirement	1 2 3 4 5 6 7 8 9 10
9. Stress	1 2 3 4 5 6 7 8 9 10
10. Sense of Well Being	1 2 3 4 5 6 7 8 9 10
Overall Assessment	**1 2 3 4 5 6 7 8 9 10**

Step 4: You may want to consider writing a One Page Life Plan using the template on the CD.

Where are the Opportunities for Improvement?

In left column: Identify key areas that influenced your assessment.
In right column: Brainstorm actions that can be taken to improve low ratings or maintain high ratings.

Problem Areas or Successes	Action to Improve or Maintain

Example for Stress:
Too much focus on work, not enough on family & fun.

Limit work to 45 hrs/week max! Put personal events on my business calendar.

VISION
MISSION
OBJECTIVES
STRATEGIES
ACTION PLANS

The Vision Statement
What are you building?

"When you are clear about what you are building, you make it easier for others to show up!"

Everybody is building something... an organization, a program, a department! Well written Vision Statements answer the question: What is being built? ...in three sentences or less!

Effective Vision Statements need not be long, but must clearly describe what you are building. A few key words will go a long way. In this section we are going to help you create a clear and compelling picture of what your non-profit will look like in 1, 3 or even 5 years.

The Vision Statement is at the top of The One Page Business Plan because readers of your plan need to quickly understand the big picture. Non-profits have been writing excellent One Page Plans since 1994 and we have a lot of examples to share with you. In this section and in Chapter 10 there are a wide variety of sample Vision Statements for non-profits, non-governmental organizations and associations. There are also sample Vision Statements for departments and retail/profit centers.   The Vision Statement templates in this section have been refined over the years and will help you quickly create a first draft.

Vision Statements answer these questions:

- What type of non-profit is this?
- What is the geographic scope?
- Who are the target recipients of the service you provide?
- What is the capacity of your organization?
- How many people will you serve?
- What are the key products, programs and services?
- What are the annual funding requirements?
- How many & what kind of employees will we need?

This exercise is designed to help you brainstorm the Who, What, Why, When, Where and How's for your Non-Profit. Review the questions, write down your initial thoughts, insights and ahas. Writing outside the boxes is allowed and encouraged.

WHAT?

Services or products? or both? How many?

Non-Profit image: What will this non-profit be known for?

Leadership Role: What is your role? How will you spend your time?

WHERE?

Non-Profit: Local, regional, national, or international?

Clients/Recipients: Where are they? What cities, states, countries?

Business Operations: Headquarters, offices, program locations, etc.?

WHO?

Clients/Recipients: Who are they? What needs do they have?

Staff: Who needs to be on your team?

Strategic Alliances: Who can you partner with?

Advisors: Who can provide professional and strategic advice and help you grow this non-profit properly?

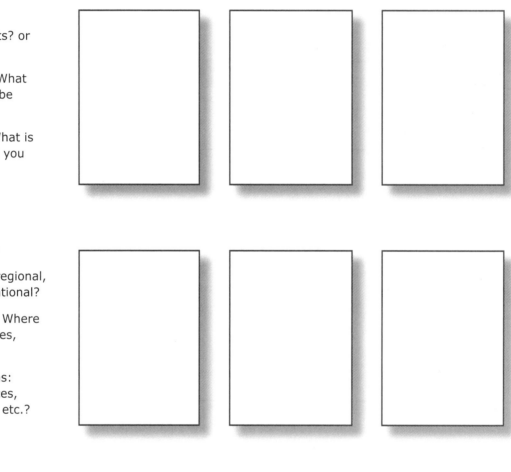
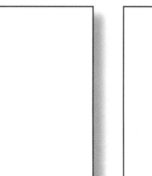

Creating the Non-Profit You Want

Don't worry about answering all of the questions; they may or may not apply to your non-profit.

WHEN?

Start-up: When will this non-profit be operational?

Facilities: When will office space be required?

Systems: When must they be selected, tested, and operational?

Staff: When will you need to hire your staff?

WHY?

Executive Director: Why am I creating this non-profit?

Clients/Recipients: Why will they use/buy these products or services?

Funding Services: Why will they fund this non-profit?

HOW?

Funding: How will this non-profit be funded?

Culture: How do you want to interact with the Board, employees, volunteers, vendors?

Personal Beliefs: How will your personal beliefs impact this non-profit?

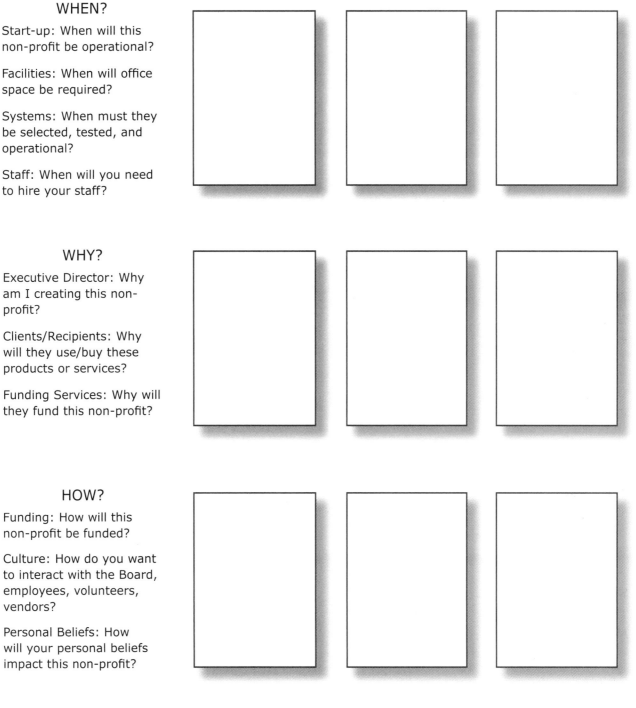

Interview Exercise

Slightly overwhelmed? Want to make the process inclusive? Invite a trusted advisor to interview you using the questions below. Have them interview you in person or over the phone. Have them ask you the questions and record your responses. You might consider doing this interview process with more than one person.

1. What's the service or product?

Describe three characteristics of your service or product:

Describe three things your service or product WON'T DO:

2. Who's the client/recipient?

Describe three characteristics of the ideal recipient of your service/product:

Describe three characteristics of clients you would be better off NOT SERVING:

3. What's the environment?

Describe three characteristics of successful non-profits you admire and WOULD like to emulate:

Describe three characteristics of non-profits you WOULD NOT like to emulate:

Crafting Your Vision Statement

Getting the first draft onto paper is always the most difficult. It is infinitely easier to edit! The fill-in-the-blank template below is geared to help you quickly create a first draft. In essence, each blank is a question; to quickly and easily create a first draft, simply fill in all the blanks! Not able to fill in all of the blanks at this time? Don't worry... complete those that you can! Revisit the blanks later, you may need to do some research or enlist the help from others.

Vision Statement

Within the next _____ years grow (the) _____
(Name of your organization/department/function/committee)

into a successfully run _____ non-profit organization with annual funding of $_____
(geographic scope)

providing _____
(describe specific services or functions)

for/to _____
(identify who will be the recipients of your services)

A Simple Formula for Writing Your Vision Statement...

Who & How Many will you Serve +
What will you Provide +
Geographical Scope +
Annual Funding Requirements

Non-Profit Vision Statements that Work

Each of the Vision Statements below paints a concise picture of what these non-profit organizations, programs or departmental functions will look like within the stated planning horizon. They also reflect the personal style of the plan's author. It is important to note that not all of them used the template that we suggest as a starting point... but that does not detract from them.

Never Too Late, Inc.	Within the next 3 years grow Never Too Late, Inc. into a national, self-supporting, successfully run non-profit organization with annual funding of $200K, providing end of life wishes and dreams on a daily basis for the forgotten elderly and terminally ill adults of all ages.
Allies in Recovery	Within the next 2 years grow Allies in Recovery into a $300,000 local not-for-profit organization providing a replicable national model of scientifically-validated training, peer support services, and treatment resources for family and friends who wish to engage in treatment to improve the recovery outcomes of their loved ones afflicted with alcohol and/or drug problems.
Burlingame Library Foundation	By year end 2008, the Burlingame Library Foundation will provide the Burlingame Library with a reliable income stream of $250,000 per year through fund raising activities, events and endowment programs. These funds will be dedicated to the Burlingame Library for the purpose of supporting programs, infrastructure and other activities that would not otherwise be funded or supported via the annual library budget.
Bay Area Entrepreneurs Association	Within five years, build BAEA into a nationally recognized micro-enterprise organization with an extensive greater San Francisco Bay Area network of entrepreneurial support groups providing nationally recognized products, programs and services to entrepreneurs, small-business owners and partner organizations.
The Wellspring Family Service Agency	Within five years we see ourselves as the premier Family Service Agency and the charity of choice among local, regional, state and national stakeholders. We see a growing funding base to include a $500,000 endowment and an operating reserve of 3 – 6 months supported by entrepreneurial revenue programs to yield a more diversified and flexible funding base. We will be recognized as the " The Can Do Will Do" organization.

Med Camps of Louisiana	By 2010 we see Med Camps of Louisiana with a $2 million annual budget, three (3) sites in Louisiana, and recognized nationwide for ADA camping compliance. We see stable funding resources, sponsored camps, year around programs, large endowment and more campers and staff. We are highly awarded and Med Camps is a household name.
Kidsteem	We are building a non-profit organization delivering out-of-school time educational enrichment programs that support school aged children in developing life skills, self esteem and confidence.
Meals on Wheels	Grow the Tri-County Meals on Wheels program into a premier nutrition service for the homeward bound elderly and disabled adults in our tri-county service area, providing a full compliment of quality prepared meals and personal attention seven days a week. Within three years we envision serving 1,500 meals everyday through a network of 500 volunteers.
Unity in Marin Spiritual Center	Our vision for Unity in Marin is to be a Spiritual Center where spirituality is practiced and experienced thru celebration, ritual, ceremony, prayer, play, study, and silence with people seeking personal and spiritual growth and transformation. This vision includes a permanent modern facility in a vibrant natural setting in central Marin County.
Shea Therapeutic Center	Within the next three years, grow the Shea Center into a preeminent $2 million organization providing therapeutic equestrian activities to a diverse community of people with special needs and providing internationally recognized education to therapeutic equestrian professionals.
Our House: A Home & A Haven	In the next 3 to 5 years we will have a $2 million budget, well paid professional staff, with a larger footprint on the block, esthetically pleasing and well maintained. We will offer a residential program, have full membership in the Children's Coalition and strong partnerships throughout the community. We will be known as experts in short term placements and have an annual signature fund raising event. We will be LANO Certified with a younger, energetic Board of Directors.
Oklahoma Jazz Hall of Fame	Within the next three years, grow the Oklahoma Jazz Hall of Fame into an international art institution with annual funding of $1.3 million, providing preservation, education and performance of jazz to music lovers.

Vision Statement for a Retail/Profit Center

Most non-profits have retail/profit centers… it is not possible to get all of the funding from grants and donations. Have each of your retail/profit centers create a One Page Business Plan. This template will jump-start the process and help create a solid first draft.

Retail/Profit Center Vision Statement Template

Within the next _____ years grow (the) _____ retail/profit center at
      (1, 3, or 5 yrs)   (retail/profit center name)

_____ into _____ generating \$_____ in sales and _____% in
   (non-profit name)   (type of business)

gross profit providing _____
                               (list 2-3 of your key products/services)

to _____.
               (list 2-3 key clients/customers)

Example

Book Store at Unity in Marin Spiritual Center

Within the next 3 years develop the Unity Book Store at Unity in Marin into a highly efficient, reliable, profitable retail book store generating $50,000 in revenues and a gross profit of at least 40% that provides spiritual books, tapes and learning aids to the members of Unity and the general public. The book store will be managed by a part-time, paid professional with 2 – 4 volunteers as necessary.

Vision Statement for a Department

If your non-profit has support functions, have each of your managers create a Vision Statement for their department. This template will make creating the first draft easy.

Department Vision Statement Template

Within the next _____ years grow _____ at _____
          (1, 3, or 5 yrs)   (department name)   (non-profit)

into a successful provider of _____
                           (describe services and/or functions)

to _____. Future capabilities/capacity
       (name internal/external customers)

will include _____.
                 (describe capabilities/capacity)

Example

Marketing Team at Unity in Marin Spiritual Center

Within the next 3 years develop the Marketing Team at Unity In Marin into a highly efficient and effective volunteer marketing team that provides pro bono services in marketing, advertising, public relations, promotions and special events services to support programs and events identified by the Board of Directors and other committees.

Vision Statement for a Project or Program

Projects and programs are the backbone of your non-profit; each of them should have their own One Page Plan. Have your Program Managers write a One Page Plan for each of their programs, this template should help them quickly draft their Vision Statement.

Project or Program Vision Statement Template

Within the next _____ months _____ _____ that
           (1 to 12)   (build/develop/complete)   (project/program name)

_____ for
       (describe project outcome in terms of new capabilities, capacity, benefits)

_____ .
       (identify users / purchasers / beneficiaries of this project)

Example

Complete a Comprehensive Communication Plan (CCP) for communicating the Dominican institutional mission by the end of the Fall 2001 semester with implementation beginning in Spring 2002. Our vision is that within five years, every student, faculty, trustee and member of staff will not only know the 4 Pillars of the Dominican Spirit, but will be living and sharing the principles of Study, Reflection, Community and Service within their extended communities.

Vision Statements that Work Together

Each department, program and committee within a non-profit should have a Vision Statement that is supportive of the overall non-profit's Vision. Listed below is a partial set of Vision Statements for the Unity in Marin Spiritual Center. Please note these Vision Statements were created by teams and committees in a very participative manner... hence the styles are very different, but collectively they paint a very clear picture of how this organization works together.

Unity in Marin Consolidated Plan	Within 2 years 500 members will attend 3 transformational Sunday services, and a mid-week, and monthly healing service. We will have an active 7 days per week spiritual center and have 100+ children in FM with 40 personal growth and spiritual education class night/events for adults per month. UIM will have 3 impactful outreach programs in Marin County and beyond. People will experience a deep sense of spiritual community, personal transformative growth and service to others as a path to God.
Sunday Services	Build highly inspiring, inclusive, transformative Worship Celebrations connecting to Spirit within one's self and others through words, music and meditation
Marketing	Build a highly efficient & effective volunteer marketing team that promotes the vision of Unity by providing public relations, advertising, promotions & mktg communication services to support programs and events identified by the Minister and the Unity Leadership Team.
Education	A full-service educational & community enrichment organization for adults, children, & families comprising basic & advanced Unity classes, serious adjunctive studies & a wide variety of community-building activities. Classes are taught by trained faculty supplemented by guest specialty-expert teachers. Special varied-format programs of commitment & growth are offered to maximize participation opportunities for seekers of all ages and family status. Community events & celebrations are offered to deepen & broaden members' connections to each other.
Events & Facility Rentals	Unity Center is a coveted site for corporate meetings, weddings, and private parties. We are known for the beauty of our site and our excellent service and technology. The event rentals program operates in harmony with UIM events and is a major source of income.
Accounting & Finance	To be an effective, spirit-guided, prosperity-conscious team that provides professional financial expertise that fosters financial prosperity for Unity In Marin, the association of Unity churches and our extended community.

Summarize

Rewrite your Vision Statement below. Use your own style to describe your vision and choose words that are comfortable and meaningful to you.

Vision Statement

_____

_____

_____

_____

_____

_____

_____

_____

Now rewrite the Vision Statement one more time in The One Page Business Plan Word Template provided on the CD at the back of the book.

Feedback Exercise

Reflect on your Vision Statement for a few days. Then consider sharing your Vision Statement with at least a couple of people and asking them for their feedback. Use this page to take notes.

First Person Feedback

Second Person Feedback

Note here key words and phrases from above or other sources you would like to use in your own Vision Statement:

VISION

MISSION

OBJECTIVES

STRATEGIES

ACTION PLANS

Mission

Why does this non-profit exist?

Every non-profit organization exists for a reason. Good Mission Statements describe not only why your organization exists, but why each of your products, programs and services exist.

Great Mission Statements are short and memorable. They communicate in just a few compelling words (6 – 8 words are ideal) the non-profit's focus and what it is committed to deliver. In the world of non-profits, the great Mission Statements make a strong appeal to our emotions.

The non-profit's Mission Statement is its promise. There are two parts to the promise; 1) who are you serving and 2) what are you committed to doing for them? When the promise is clearly defined and articulated it will attract the people you serve, and it will define the culture within your organization.

A well-constructed Mission Statement will not only attract the people you serve, but it can also attract your Board of Directors, management team, employees, vendors, volunteers, donors and funders. Attracting the wrong people? Can't get the right kind of volunteers, donors or funders? Maybe your Mission Statement does not truly reflect why your organization exists.

The work of your non-profit is important. Take the time to create a powerful Mission Statement that helps the world know what you do! Use it to make strategic and critical decisions! Use it to create the culture that is critical to your success. And keep it short and memorable! Everyone involved in your non-profit needs to be able to state your Mission Statement without blinking their eyes!

Mission Statements answer these specific questions:

- Why does this non-profit organization exist?
- Who are we committed to serve?
- What human, social or environmental tragedy are we helping to solve?
- What are we committed to providing?
- What promise are we making?

"Mission Statements always answer the question:

Who will we serve and what will we do for them?"

Believe it or not... you have a choice as to who you work with! Consider these questions:

- Who do you want to work with?
- What causes/issues are important to you?
- What problems can you solve?
- Who is currently working with your ideal client?

- Where are the people you want to serve?
- What work gives you professional satisfaction?
- Who has the resources to pay your fees?
- Who makes you smile?

Exercise instructions:

1. In the center circle, describe the people, groups or organizations you want to work with. These people have faces! What do they look like? What do they need help with? The more specific you can be... the easier it will be for you to find them, and vice-versa.

2. In the outer circle, list the people and/or communities that know your existing and/or future clients. These people need to know you exist; they can introduce you to those that need your service.

Put a Face on your Future Clients

- Age
- Gender
- Race
- Cause
- Issue/Need
- Geography
- Economic Status

When you are clear about who you want to serve, you make it easier for them to find you!

And Why?

Why will clients/recipients use/buy your services/products? What value do these services or products provide the client? What unique benefits do these services or products provide the client/recipient?

What passion(s) are you trying to satisfy by building this non-profit? What beliefs do you have about this cause or need that will impact this non-profit? What is the highest good that this non-profit can achieve? What values will drive this organization? Who will benefit from this work?

 **Crafting Your Mission Statement**

Experiment with 1 – 8 key words that describe why your Organization, Program, Committee or Function exists from your client's/donors/community's point of view. Why will your clients or donors participate in your programs or come to your events or donate to your organization?

Why does this non-profit exist?

1st Attempt:

2nd Attempt:

A Simple Formula for Writing Your Mission Statement...

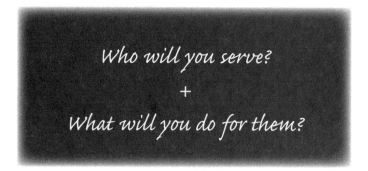

Who will you serve?
+
What will you do for them?

Examples of Mission Statements

The best Mission Statements are short and memorable! And eight (8) words or less!

They also may evoke an emotional response, particularly given the nature of people helping other people in need. Well written Mission Statements will attract those people that need your services and attract those that want to volunteer, fund and work for your non-profit. Your Mission Statement should focus everyone involved with your non-profit on the critical nature of the work to be done!

As you review these Mission Statements, ask yourself how well do they answer the question, "Why does this Non-Profit exist?" Notice which ones you are personally drawn to, and why!

Nature Conservancy	Helping to save the last great places on earth.
Never Too Late Inc.	Touching Lives – Making Magical Moments Happen Now!
Kidsteem	Create innovative educational enrichment programs for children and their families.
Volunteer Center of NW Suburban Chicago	Enrich Lives through Community Volunteerism.
Allies in Recovery	Providing skills & resources to family and friends to manage addiction.
YWCA	We build strong kids, strong families, strong communities.
Pro-Attitude	End stress through a shift in attitude.
Unity Church	Discover Divinity Within and Reach Out in Loving Service.
No. Illinois Food Bank	We work with food for people without food.

Interview Exercise

If you prefer to interactively work with an individual or group on creating your Mission Statement, have an interviewer ask you these questions, and have them write down your responses. Use the right column to restate what the interviewer heard, in your words.

The Interviewer	You
1. Why will clients/recipients use your service or product?	Answer restated:
2. What is your organization committed to providing your clients?	Answer restated:
3. What can your non-profit promise?	Answer restated:
4. What passion(s) are you trying to satisfy by building this non-profit?	Answer restated:

More Sample Mission Statements

Center for Community Benefit Organization	Building the Professional Capacity of Non-Profit Organizations in the East Bay.
Head Start	Provide opportunities for parents and children to be successful.
Shea Therapeutic Center	Improving the lives of people with disabilities through therapeutic horse-related programs.
Jewish Vocational Services, San Francisco	Bring People and Work Together.
The Ritter Center	The Marin County Safety Net.
Our House	Providing Immediate Help to Youth.
The Wellspring: Family Service Agency	To strengthen and value the family through direct service, education, advocacy and women's leadership.
Hospital Engineering Dept.	Build the right projects, and build the projects right.
California Nurses Association	A Voice for Nurses... A Vision for Healthcare.
Sacramento Waste Mgt.	Help us lose weight. Recycle Monthly!
Just Say Yes	Educate, equip, train & support "Young" Internet-based entrepreneurs.

Summarize

Rewrite your Mission Statement below. Experiment with different adjectives and verbs. It may help to move on to another section and come back to summarize your Mission Statement.

Mission Statement

_____

_____

_____

_____

_____

_____

_____

_____

 Now type your Mission Statement into The One Page Business Plan Word Template provided on the CD at the back of the book.

THE ONE PAGE BUSINESS PLAN

Feedback Exercise

Review your Mission Statement on page 52 or 56 and the examples on pages 53 and 55. Is yours too long? Unclear? Refine your Mission Statement below and then discuss it with at least two people. Use their feedback to complete your final version.

Use the examples on the preceding pages to help you refine your Mission Statement:

First Person Feedback

Second Person Feedback

VISION
MISSION
OBJECTIVES
STRATEGIES
ACTION PLANS

Objectives

What will be measured?

"Well defined goals focus people, budgets and resources on the right things!"

Objectives are short statements that quantify the end results or outcomes of any work effort. Good Objectives are easy to write and are instantly recognizable. They answer the question "What will we measure?"

Objectives clarify what you are trying to accomplish in specific, measurable terms. For an Objective to be effective, it needs to be a well-defined target with quantifiable elements. It is important to include different types of Objectives that cover the entire scope of your organization.

Well Conceived Objectives:

- Define success or outcomes in a measurable manner
- Provide a quantitative pulse of the non-profit
- Focus resources towards specific results
- Give people/organizations specific targets to aim for
- Establish a framework for accountability and incentive pay
- Minimize subjectivity and emotionalism
- Measure the end results of work effort

Although there is no magical number of Objectives, a One Page Business Plan can accommodate nine. Consider an Objective for funding or revenue, expenses and reserve. The remainder of the Objectives can be used to define program goals, process measures, employee development, and other important goals that are critical to your success.

Objectives Must be Graphable

The One Page methodology makes writing Objectives simple... All Objectives must be graphable!

Managers learn early in their careers that what you measure is what gets improved. In your organization undoubtedly you have charts that measure and track specific outcomes by project, program and function.

Charts are great... everybody can read charts. It's obvious when you are ahead of goal or not!

The key to setting meaningful Objectives is to identify goals which are:

- critical to your success and
- can be easily tracked

(*Easily tracked = data is readily available & the specific target can be counted*)

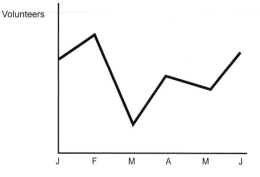

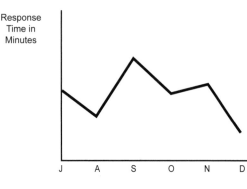

Stated very simply, if you can not count it over time (easily)... it's not an Objective. On the Crafting Objectives exercise, we provide you with many frequently used goals... please note, all of them are graphable!

It's easy to craft meaningful Objectives when you use these 3 simple guidelines:

- Write only Objectives that can be graphed
- Include a numerical value in every Objective
- Assign a name & date to assure accountability

Final thought: It is not unusual for this way of measurement to result in an overhaul of an organization's data collection. Frequently we don't collect the information that is the most important.

A Simple Formula for Writing Objectives...

Action To Be Taken

+

Something Countable

+

Target/Completion Date

Here are some examples using this formula:

- Increase the number of hot meals delivered from 125 to 200 per day by 12/31.

- Achieve 75% city-wide recycling rate by 2010.

- Reduce high school dropout rate from 18% to less than 5% by 2008.

- Increase after-school library usage from 30 to 100 students by November 30th.

- Add 110 new adult learners to ESL classes this year; 40 in 1st half, 30 in Q3 & 40 in Q4

- Reduce teen-age pregnancy from 22% to less than 10% by 2007.

- Increase average donations per individual from $60 to $100 per year.

- Reduce cost of delivering meals from $22 to $15 through better scheduling of routes.

- Increase total Opera ticket revenues from $700,000 to $1 million.

- Sell 300 "Kids are Winners" t-shirts and caps by March 15th.

- Pickup 10 tons of trash on Earth Day weekend.

brainstorm
Where Does Success Come From?

Where does success come from? What will it look like? Think about your past experiences, what you have learned from these, and answer the questions on the left. Imagine what your future success will look like and respond to the questions on the right.

Where have you been successful in the past? or Where has your non-profit been successful in the past?	How can you expand upon these successes?
What were your past mistakes? Mistakes your organization has made?	What have you learned from these mistakes?
What ideas have you not acted on?	Which of these ideas will you go forward with?

What Do We Want to Celebrate?

What accomplishments would you like to celebrate? Brainstorm three significant accomplishments you would like to be celebrating at the end of this year and next year.

This year?

Next year?

Imagine what you might say at the annual celebration dinner:

CONGRATULATIONS!

"We successfully completed (........)."

"We are proud to announce the beginning of (........)."

"We no longer have to deal with (........) because we (........)."

"We increased (........) by (........)."

"We decreased (........) by (........)."

"Our services helped (........) people this year!"

Sample Objectives...

Listed below are six sets of Objectives, from very different non-profits. These are the "measures of success" they have selected to monitor and track monthly. Some are rather traditional, others are not.

Alzheimer's Care Clinic

- Provide services to 350 individuals who have Alzheimer's or a related dementia.
- Provide case management services to 180 individuals in tri-county area.
- Provide Ombudsman services in Tri-County; 4,800 contacts with residents.
- Operate the San Martin Metro Adult Day Support Center at 35 average daily census.
- Operate the Adult Day Support Center at 26 average daily census.
- Serve 110,000 meals through the Meals on Wheels Program.
- Serve 1,000 seniors at the Metro Senior Center.
- Increase fee-for-service revenue to $525,000; 25% above last year.
- Obtain additional $125,000 in Foundation funding.

Meals on Wheels

- Provide services to 475 homebound elderly each month.
- Provide expanded nutritional service products to 300 individuals.
- Add new customers at the rate of 45 per month.
- Increase case management revenue to an average of $2,500 per month.
- Recruit and train 25 new route drivers, both volunteer and paid.
- Obtain $80,000 in county contract and foundation funding.
- Provide 12 in-service training sessions for route drivers and 24 for MoW staff.
- Provide nutrition services to 75 disabled adults each month.

Bay Area Entrepreneur Association

- Increase membership from 150 to 300 by 12/31/06.
- Launch 2 networks by 6/2006 and add 3 more networks by 6/2007.
- Generate $8,000 from entrepreneurial programs, events and products in FY 2006.
- Host 3 regional network events with at least 50 attendees each and generate $3,000.
- Conduct 4 workshops/programs with an average of 25 participants and generate $4,000.
- Increase low-income members to 25 and increase minority members 25% by 3/2006.
- Award 5 scholarships totaling $1,300 in FY 2006.
- Recognize 10 entrepreneurs for outstanding business growth & community service in FY2006.

Notice that all of these Objectives contain a numerical value that is graphable! This is critical.

Volunteer Fire Department

- Reduce fire response time to 5 minutes average by 12/31.
- Reduce freeway emergency response time to 7 minutes average by 12/31.
- Reduce loss of property by 12% from previous year.
- Assure there is no more than a 5% deviation from last year's monthly overtime budget.
- Reduce worker injuries to no more than 6 per month by 12/31.
- 60% employees involved in participation activities by 7/01.

Oklahoma Jazz Hall of Fame

- Increase Revenue from $434,947 to $500,000.
- Increase Surplus from $44,878 to $55,000.
- Increase membership from 400 to 600.
- Increase performances revenue from $77,000 to $123,000.
- Increase donations from $374,884 to $750,000.
- Increase grants from $259,784 to $520,000.
- Increase educational program from 3 to 5 & scholarships from four to eight.
- Increase staff from 2 to 6.
- Increase volunteers from 15 to 50.

Unity in Marin, Spiritual Center

- Increase Sunday attendance from 220 to 400 by December 31, 2006.
- Increase annual income from $380,000 to $620,000
- Increase Youth Education weekly attendance from 15 average to 40 average.
- Increase new membership from 75 to 100.
- Increase average Adult Education class enrollment from 12 to 25.
- Increase Spring and Fall in-home program from 100/150 to 180/220.
- Increase Service Ministry involvement from 105 to 150.

Listed below are templates for Objectives that are fairly common for Non-Profits. They are designed to help you create a first draft. It is possible, but not likely all of these templates will work for your organization.

Financial

Revenue
Achieve 2007 _____ revenue of $ _____.

Funding*
Increase _____ funding from $ _____ to $ _____.

Operating Expense
Increase (reduce) Operating Expenses from $ _____ to $ _____.

Cost of Services
Reduce cost of _____ product/service from _____ to _____ by _____ (date).

Accounts Receivable
Reduce # of average days outstanding from _____ to _____ by _____ (date).

Client/Recipient

New Clients/Recipients/Members
In 2007 increase number of _____ served from _____ to _____.

Units Served/Sold
Increase number of _____ served/sold from _____ to _____.

Workshops/Programs
Increase number of _____ workshops/programs from _____ to _____.

Initial Usage
Increase initial usage of _____ from _____ to _____.

Outcomes
Increase client/recipient satisfaction from _____ to _____.

*Suggestions: grants, donations, endowments, sponsorship, dues

If you do not see a template for an Objective that you need, create your own using the others as a model. Note: These are the four categories of the Balanced Scorecard.

Process Improvement

Success Rates
Increase _____ success rate from _____ to _____.

Error Rates
Decrease _____ error rates from _____ to _____.

Productivity & Effectiveness*
Increase _____ productivity from _____ to _____.

Customer Service
Improve _____ program's _____ performance from _____ to _____.

Response Rates
Increase _____ response rate from _____ % to _____ %.

Learning & Growth

Skill Improvement*
Increase # of employees capable of _____ (function) from _____ to _____.

Resource Utilization
Improve _____ (resource) utilization from _____ to _____.

Output per Employee*
Increase _____ per employee from _____ to _____ ($, %, numerical value).

Waste/Inefficiencies
Reduce _____ waste from $ _____ to $ _____ (could be %).

Retention
Increase staff (or volunteer) retention from _____ to _____.

*Alternatives: Board, manager, staff, volunteers, 3rd party resources

Summarize your Objectives

Transfer your Objectives you created on pages 66 and 67 to this worksheet or directly into The One Page Business Plan template provided on the CD at the back of the book. If you need to create additional Objectives do so now. Remember you can only have nine Objectives on your One Page Plan.

1

2

3

4

5

6

7

8

9

Feedback Exercise

Share your Objectives with at least two other people. Ask them if these are the most important things for you and your team to track and monitor throughout the year. Use their feedback to fine-tune your Objectives.

First Person Feedback	Second Person Feedback

VISION
MISSION
OBJECTIVES
STRATEGIES
ACTION PLANS

Strategies

How will this non-profit be built?

"Following a predefined set of strategies is critical to keeping a non-profit on track."

Success is rarely an accident. It is usually the result of executing a carefully crafted set of strategies. Strategies provide a blueprint or road map for building and managing an organization. They also provide a comprehensive overview of the business models and best practices and frequently say as much about what the non-profit will not do, as what it will do.

Strategies set the direction, philosophy, values, and methodology for building and managing your non-profit. They establish guidelines and boundaries for critical decisions. Following a predefined set of strategies is critical to keeping a non-profit on track.

One way of understanding strategies is to think of them as industry practices. Every industry has its leaders, its followers, and its rebels, and each has an approach for capturing market share. Pay attention to the successful non-profits in your industry and you can learn important lessons. You can also learn a lot from their failures.

Strategies are not secret. In fact they are common knowledge and openly shared in every industry. Pick up any industry's publication and you will know precisely what the industry's leaders have to say about the opportunities and how to capitalize on them. These leaders will also share their current problems and their solutions. This can be critical information for building and managing your non-profit. Study what the best of the best are doing... and incorporate those practices which will make your organization stronger and more effective. Add your unique solutions, processes and techniques, and you will have a powerful set of strategies to move your non-profit forward.

In summary, Strategies are broad statements, covering multiple years that:

- Set the direction, philosophy, values
- Define the business model, business practices & culture
- Establish guidelines for evaluating important decisions
- Set limits on what a non-profit will do or will not do

There are many moving parts to a successful non-profit organization... and most of them have to work extraordinarily well in order for the mission to be accomplished. Additionally, non-profits rarely have the budgets and resources that for-profit businesses do, so they must be more creative. It is also critical that non-profits learn from each other!

This exercise is meant to have you think about your non-profit from a holistic or 360° perspective. Review this list; use it as a catalyst to think about what will actually be necessary to make your non-profit successful over time... and/or what will be required to move it to the next level of success. As you are crafting your Strategies on page 80-81, you may want to refer back to this page.

☐ Personal Expertise	☐ Grants & Donations	☐ Board of Directors
☐ Technical Knowledge	☐ Fee for Services	☐ Management Team
☐ Professional Reputation	☐ Risk Mgt./Insurance	☐ Employees
☐ Capabilities & Capacity	☐ Publishing: Self or Trade	☐ Volunteers
☐ Market Presence	☐ Speaking: Free or Paid	☐ Referral Sources
☐ Uniqueness of Offering	☐ Build, Buy or Partner	☐ Strategic Alliances
☐ Branding	☐ Licensing & Franchising	☐ Use of Technology
☐ Value Proposition	☐ Support Services	☐ Facilities: Rent or Buy
☐ Pricing	☐ Productizing your Services	☐ Loans or Capital
☐ Importance of Quality	☐ Hi or Low Tech Products	☐ Amount of Travel
☐ Availability & Access	☐ Trademarks/Patents	☐ Family Support
☐ Geographical Area Served	☐ Customer Service	☐ Peace of Mind
☐ Government Compliance	☐ Governance	☐ Amount of free time

Deciding Which Strategies Are Appropriate for Your Non-Profit

Finding appropriate strategies for your non-profit is not difficult. Much information is readily available to you for free or at minimal cost. Selecting strategies you can utilize is also not difficult.

Where do you find strategies specific to your non-profit? Foundations, technical assistance providers, and countless publications & articles put out by nationally recognized experts are a great place to start.

These publications are filled with current articles on industry trends in the critical areas of fund development, marketing, finance and operations. They are usually short and concise. They describe the problems and opportunities with which the industry is struggling and the solutions that non-profits are implementing.

A review of the contents for the last few issues will certainly give you a solid perspective on what's important in your industry and how the leading edge non-profits are planning their futures.

If you are starting a non-profit, you'll have access to some important information that you will want to seriously consider before proceeding. Also, if this is a new non-profit, and it requires funding, you can be sure the funder/lender will want to know how you are planning to address these issues.

Other people that know your non-profit can be very helpful in identifying and selecting strategies. Your Board, banker, CPA, attorney, vendors, employees, and the recipients of your services have a lot of insight into your non-profit. Ask them for their thoughts.

Industry Research Exercise

Review the last three issues of your industry's trade, professional or association journals and answer the questions below.

What and where are the opportunities?	How can you capitalize on them?
What threats exist?	**How can we minimize the threats or turn the threats into opportunities?**

Examples of Issues Affecting Non-Profits

competition for funding	staff turnover
revenue generation	government regulations
contract fulfillment	board governance
technology	management talent
affordability	

What's working in your Non-Profit?

It's just as important to know what works in your non-profit as what doesn't. Use the keywords list at the bottom to help you brainstorm if you get stuck (for established non-profits only.)

What currently works well at our non-profit?	How can we improve?
What doesn't work well?	**How do we solve the problems?**

management	internal controls	communication
employees	service/product quality	inventory management
board of directors	service capacity	customer service
facilities	flexibility	safety
employee benefits	yields	profit margin
overtime	expense control	morale

Critical Issues
Examination

Select three critical issues that are limiting your non-profit's effectiveness or financial health. This exercise helps you differentiate between symptoms and root causes so that you can see more clearly what needs to happen to achieve a permanent and effective change (for established non-profits only.)

List 3 issues or symptoms:	What is the root cause of this?	What needs to change?	How will results be measured?
EXAMPLE Complaints from walk-ins	Poorly trained intake staff	Simplify admissions process	Count # of complaints & compliments

A Simple Formula for Writing Strategies...

Define business activity

+

Expected Results

+

How it will be done

In most industries there are four to six core strategies that the most successful businesses follow. These core strategies are easy to understand, remain relatively constant over time, are used by market leaders, and result in growth and profitability. The same is true for non-profits.

Great strategy statements can be broad and yet create tremendous focus. When you have the right strategies for your non-profit, they will probably last for several years with minor changes. A significant breakthrough in your industry, or a significant change in a key program, can cause you to revisit your strategies.

Strategies must address both internal and external influences that are affecting or may affect your non-profit. External strategies capitalize on opportunities to grow the non-profit or overcome outside threats. Internal strategies address issues related to the organization's strengths and weaknesses in the areas of culture, capacity, capabilities, efficiency, and profitability.

Strategies for the 21st Century

Elevate Volunteerism
Retiring baby-boomers want to stay active and contribute. Don't waste their talents on licking stamps and stuffing envelopes. Use their professional skills wisely.

Be Accountable!
The dot-com boom spawned lots of new philanthropists; but their money came with the requirement to track and score specific outcomes. Can you prove your outcomes?

Consolidate & Merge to Survive
There are about 1.5 million non-profits in the U.S. – more than 80% of them operate with budgets of less than $100,000 per year. Who can you merge or partner with to increase your effectiveness?

Develop Next Generation Leaders
The senior executive pool is retiring; future shortage of managers is inevitable. Be creative! New thinking will be required!

brainstorm EXERCISE

We call this exercise Bend the Curve. Step 1: Draft an Objective for Fund Development.
Step 2: Brainstorm up to four Strategies that have the capability to significantly increase your funding over the next 3 – 5 years. Step 3: Identify 2 – 4 key Action Plans per Strategy. Action Plans are typically Projects or Programs.

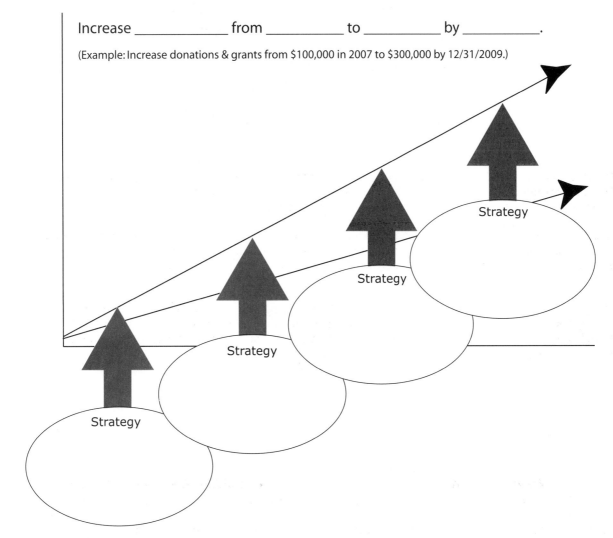

Increase _____ from _____ to _____ by _____.

(Example: Increase donations & grants from $100,000 in 2007 to $300,000 by 12/31/2009.)

Strategy

Strategy

Strategy

Strategy

Brainstorm the 2 or 3 projects or programs that will implement the Strategies:

_____   _____   _____   _____

_____   _____   _____   _____

_____   _____   _____   _____

Sample Strategies...

Listed below are six sets of Strategies, from very different non-profits. These Strategies answer the question "what will make this non-profit successful over time".

Oklahoma Jazz Hall of Fame

- Increase revenues and surplus by promoting performances, galas & space rental.
- Build/attract membership base by promotion, advertising & organization.
- Increase performance revenue by offering diverse programming, increasing frequency & mktg.
- Build donations by dev a capital campaign plan, hiring a dev consultant and a grant writer.
- Engage and educate youth by use of library, computers & practices.
- Expand scholarship endowment by corporate & individual donations & grants.
- Improve Board effectiveness by targeted recruiting, pre-eval. & involvement through planning.
- Hire world-class staff by developing specific job descs. for key staff, recruiting and selection.
- Attract/retain volunteer base by membership, marketing & external programs.

Shea Therapeutic Equestrian Center

- Core services include therapeutic riding, hippotherapy, and non-mounted activities.
- Raise capital funds using new campaign committee.
- Redesign and staff annual fund and face-to-face giving program.
- Increase public awareness through community speaking and media relations.
- Develop campaign prospects through new Board connections.
- Maintain development focus thru weekly review mtgs.
- Develop more effective budget, cost control, reporting systems.
- Expand ED involvement in developing prospects, solicitation and stewardship.

Volunteer Fire Department

- Involve community in neighborhood targeted life and safety program.
- Involve all personnel in every aspect of life and fire safety at their locations.
- Establish and enforce performance based accountability system at all department levels.
- Establish and provide professional growth and opportunity programs for all personnel.
- Coordinate with other agencies to meet emergency response standards.
- Deliver safety education & other services within our mission to the community.
- Aggressively work to prevent hazardous conditions.
- Respond promptly to rescues, fires, medical emergencies and natural disasters.
- Ensure safe, professional, environmentally harmonious actions.

Notice that the Strategies are a combination of best-practices, business models, culture and cumulative learning... and how much information can be shared in so few words!

Bay Area Entrepreneur Association

- Use public relations and media to share successes, educate, recruit and fund.
- Market and sell BAEA endorsed products and services nationally.
- Collaborate with nat'l micro-enterprise org. in nat'l awareness programs and funding.
- Establish BAEA center to create long-term community presence & financial asset base.
- Enlist key community leaders and businesses to launch and develop new networks.
- Attract/retain low-income entrepreneurs by offering scholarships funded by corp. sponsors.
- Utilize multi-lingual/cultural programs to attract minority entrepreneurs.
- Package successful BAEA programs & products to sell to other micro-enterprise orgs.
- Use technology to manage growth, streamline ops., and deliver programs, & sell products.

Just Say Yes - Educational Technology Foundation

- Identify most successful Internet entrepreneurs thru fun One Page Bus. Plan™ contests.
- Teach students to write Internet biz plans, design sites, & conduct profitable e-commerce
- Extensively use video conferencing to mentor, train, recognize and foster YES spirit.
- Establish Internet Entrepreneur Clubs at high schools, colleges, youth clubs & org.
- Build "Just Say YES" into an int'l brand name at high schools & colleges worldwide.
- Fund foundation thru donations, corp. sponsors, product sales, Internet stock options.
- Provide inexpensive turn-key business web sites equipped with e-commerce.

Unity in Marin, Spiritual Center

- Bld upon successful Sunday Celebration: enhance music & pre/post service experience.
- Meet goals of FIA/CC/LegacyEndow/other profit-making events thru excellence in execution.
- Bld Edu. success by increased variety/continuity & excel in curric & teachers.
- Deepen prayer consciousness by expanding role of chaplains, outreach and education.
- Bld membership by better marketing & outreach prog. & congreg. involve.
- Bld upon MLT success by inviting/recognizing/coaching/thanking excellence in leadership.
- Leverage minister's time by evolving staff and leadership teams.

Crafting Your Strategies

Listed below are a set of Strategy templates designed to help you quickly create a first draft. It is unlikely your organization will need all of these Strategies... but many of them will be appropriate.

Clients/Recipients

Positioning
Become locally/nationally/internationally known for _____.

Markets & Communities Served
Focus on serving _____, _____ & _____ clients/communities.

Services/Products
Core offerings are _____, _____ & _____.

Client & Member Acquisition
Build client base by _____, _____ & _____.

Quality & Consistency
Assure quality & consistency of our programs by _____, _____ & _____.

Process Improvement

Service Delivery
Improve service delivery by _____, _____ & _____.

Revenue & Fund Development
Improve fund development by _____, _____ & _____.

Internet/Technology
Use Internet/Technology to _____, _____ & _____.

Strategic Alliances/Community Partners
Use strategic alliances to _____, _____ & _____.

Infrastructure*
Develop/Improve _____ infrastructure by _____, _____ & _____.

*people, processes, equipment, facilities

Also, be sure to review your exercises from pages 72 - 77; there may be important Strategies you identified there that are not in these templates.

Funding
Fund organization by _____, _____ & _____.

Revenue Model
Generate revenues by _____, _____ & _____.

Initial Donations/Grants/Endowments
Generate first-time donations by _____, _____ & _____.

Ongoing Revenue
Generate repeat donations/grants by _____, _____ & _____.

Cost Effectiveness & Reserves
Assure our money is spent wisely by _____, _____ & _____.

Learning & Growth

Culture
Improve our _____ culture by _____ & _____.

Board Development
Improve Board effectiveness by _____, _____ & _____.

Management Team
Attract/retain/improve key employees by _____, _____ & _____.

Staff Efficiency
Improve staff efficiency by _____, _____ & _____.

Volunteer Effectiveness
Improve volunteer effectiveness by _____, _____ & _____.

Summarize your Strategies

Transfer the Strategies you created on pages 80 and 81 to this worksheet or directly into The One Page Business Plan template provided on the CD. If you need to create additional Strategies add them to this worksheet. Remember you can only have nine Strategies on your One Page Plan.

1

2

3

4

5

6

7

8

9

Feedback Exercise

Share your Strategies with at least two other people that can give you their objective opinion. Ask them if this set of strategies will make your non-profit successful over time. Use their feedback to fine-tune your Strategies.

First Person Feedback	Second Person Feedback

VISION
MISSION
OBJECTIVES
STRATEGIES
ACTION PLANS

Action Plans

What is the work to be done?

"Major initiatives always compete with the daily fire fights!

Commit to 1-4 major projects per year. They will serve you well!"

Action Plans define the actual work to be done... the specific actions the organization must take to implement Strategies and to achieve the Objectives.

For Organization, Retail/Profit Center or Department business plans, the Action Plans will be major capacity building or infrastructure projects. These projects typically have significant capital and expense budgets associated with them, and will take multiple months to complete.

For Programs, Projects or smaller departments, the Action Plans may also have capital or expense budgets, but they are typically written to define significant ONE-TIME Projects that provide additional capabilities or capacity.

In well-written One Page Business Plans, Action Plans are NEVER "job description tasks".

Ideally, each Action Plan statement relates to an Objective or a Strategy... but it is not necessary to write an Action Plan for each and every Objective or Strategy in your One Page Business Plan. You will not have enough space. Your One Page Plan will accommodate up to 9 major plans. We suggest you craft no more than two plans per quarter.

Remember: Your One Page Business Plan is designed to capture the most important elements of your plan... not all of the elements. If you find that nine (9) Action Plans is not enough, it's possible you may need to write a separate One Page Plan for one or more of the larger programs or projects.

"Work" may be defined three ways:

- Major funding or capacity building projects or programs
- Significant infrastructure projects
- Programs/Projects that bend the curves and/or trend lines

A Simple Formula for Writing Action Plans...

Description of Work + Completion Date = Plan

Here are some examples using the formula:

- Complete the "Elder Care Made Easy" book by March 31, 2007; 1st print run by May 31st.
- Launch Q2 Project Management Series w/ "Stress-Free Project Management" on April 15th.
- Complete re-design of website with automated enrollment capabilities by July 31st.
- Build prototype web application to simplify "service surveys" by Oct. 31st.
- Hire part-time administrative assistant by February 28th; Bookkeeper by April 30th.

Work "Bends" the Curve... Project Prioritization

In the Strategy section we used the "Bend the Curve" visual to identify the major opportunities that have the potential to significantly increase fund development over the next 3 – 5 years. We can again use this visual model to help identify and prioritize the major projects, programs and initiatives you and your team are going to focus on in the next twelve months to improve capacity, capabilities, effectiveness, and efficiencies.

Critical note: This exercise may be one of the most important exercises in this book! The identification of "what you are going to improve" and "how and when you are going to do it" is central to your planning efforts. This exercise defines "the critical work" to be done in your Non-Profit over the next twelve months.

When you have agreed on the projects that will bend the curve, assign completion dates and responsibility... then craft the Action Plans. Each of these projects is a potential candidate for your One Page Business Plan! Also be sure to calculate the expense and capital budgets for these projects and get them into your One Page Budget Worksheet, which is included in the Non-Profit Tool Kit CD.

THE ONE PAGE BUSINESS PLAN

Bend the Curve
Projects that Produce Results

Identify 2 - 4 projects or programs you are going to implement this year that have the greatest potential for Bending the Capacity, Capabilities, Effectiveness, or Efficiency Curve(s) in your Non-Profit. Suggestion: Go back to page 26 and review your assessment; those functional areas with low ratings are good candidates. Brainstorm the 2 - 4 projects that have the potential to significantly improve performance. Note: Significant issues may warrant their own "Bend the Curve" worksheet.

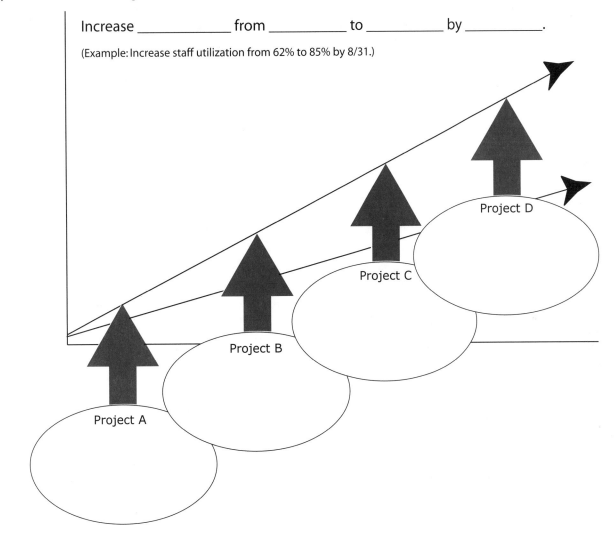

Increase _____ from _____ to _____ by _____.

(Example: Increase staff utilization from 62% to 85% by 8/31.)

Project A

Project B

Project C

Project D

Resources Required: People, Expense Budget, Capital Budget

_____   _____   _____   _____

_____   _____   _____   _____

_____   _____   _____   _____

The One Page Planning Wheel

The One Page Planning Wheel is a visual tool that helps managers and teams visualize the timing and prioritizing of key projects over the entire year.

Most managers have little problem identifying critical tasks and near-term projects that need to be completed in the next six days... or six weeks. But the identification, prioritization and calendaring of significant projects and programs in the second half of the year... or beyond, can be difficult when so frequently the focus is on short term results.

Use The One Page Planning Wheel as a tool to brainstorm the key projects in your organization, division, department or program. In the brainstorming phase, identify all major projects, then refine the list down to two or three projects per quarter.

Remember, your One Page Business Plan can accommodate up to nine (9) Action Plans.

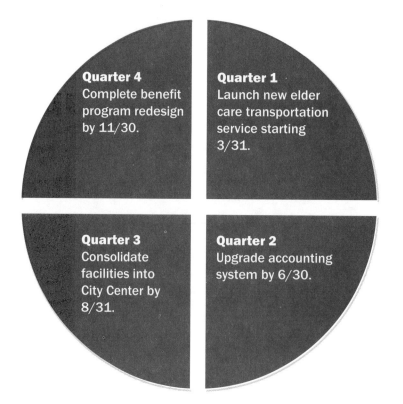

Quarter 4
Complete benefit program redesign by 11/30.

Quarter 1
Launch new elder care transportation service starting 3/31.

Quarter 3
Consolidate facilities into City Center by 8/31.

Quarter 2
Upgrade accounting system by 6/30.

The One Page Planning Wheel™

There are four quarters in a year. List one or two major organization or capacity building projects your organization, department or program must accomplish in each of the next four quarters in order to implement your strategies and achieve your overall goals.

Remember... Time exists so that everything doesn't have to happen at once!

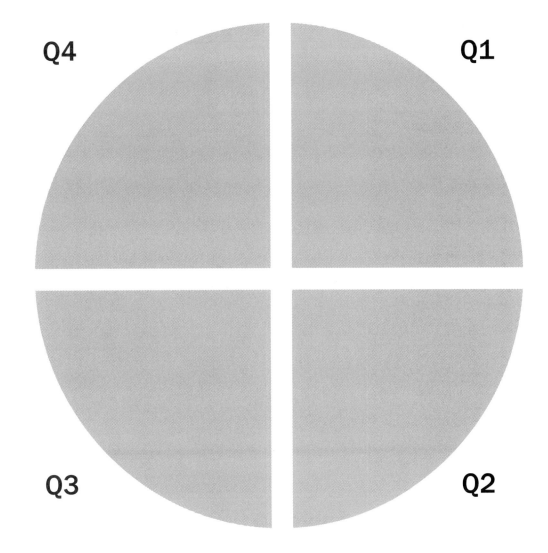

Summarize your Action Plans

Transfer the Action Plans you crafted on page 89 to this worksheet or directly into The One Page Business Plan template provided on the CD. If you need to create additional Action Plans, add them to this worksheet. Remember, you may only have nine (9) Action Plans on your One Page Plan.

1

2

3

4

5

6

7

8

9

Feedback Exercise

Share your Action Plans with at least two other people that can give you their objective opinion. Ask them if this set of Action Plans is the right set of major projects and programs for your non-profit to apply resources to in this next year. Use their feedback to fine-tune your Action Plans.

First Person Feedback	Second Person Feedback

Assembling and Polishing the Plan

"Congratulations! Your Plan is Now in Writing... What's Next?"

Assemble Your Plan onto One Page!

Select one of The One Page Business Plan templates from the Non-Profit Tool Kit CD and type in each of the five elements of the plan you created using the various exercises.

Step Back and Review Your Plan

How does it look to you? If you are like most people, some parts of your plan will be complete, while other parts will still need editing and additional detail. Don't rush the process! Make the obvious changes now, but allow some time to reflect on your plan.

Carry the plan with you; it's only one page! As new ideas and insights appear, capture them on paper. Review the Editing and Polishing suggestions on the next page. Most people find it takes about three drafts to get their plans in solid shape... don't cut the process short. Too much depends on it.

Review Your Plan with Others

You have a plan... now review it with your partners, staff, team, trusted advisors, and Board. Have them ask you clarifying questions. Take good notes on the feedback; you might consider recording the feedback sessions. Update your plan with the feedback you decide is appropriate.

Have Strategic Partners? Employees? Have them Create their One Page Business Plan

Executives, managers, teams and partners are expensive! After you have reviewed your plan with your team, and they have had a chance to ask clarifying questions, give them 3 – 7 business days to create their One Page Business Plan. Encourage them to work together; the plans will be more cohesive as a result.

Balance and Align the Plans

Balancing the plans is a process that ensures all of the functions within your organization will be working together, on the right projects and programs, in the proper sequence, at the right time... and not at cross purposes.

When your organization's plans are balanced and aligned... you can have everyone, literally, working on the same page!

Editing and Polishing the Plan

Here is a list of ideas and tips to polish your plan:

Overall Review

- Does your Vision Statement describe what you are building?
- Will your Mission Statement attract new funding? The right clients? Drive employee behavior? Is it memorable?
- Are your Objectives measurable, dated and graphable?
- Do your Strategies describe what will make your non-profit successful over time?
- Are your Action Plans significant capacity building projects? Will they achieve your Objectives? Improve performance?

Order and Abbreviation

- Edit Objectives, Strategies, and Action Plan statements to one line.
- Eliminate all unnecessary words and phrases.
- Abbreviate words when necessary.
- Use symbols like "&" in lieu of "and" to save space.
- Use "k" or "m" for thousands and "M" for millions.
- Communicate priority of Objectives, Strategies, and Action Plans by placing them in the proper order.

Creative Considerations

- Use bullets to make key points stand out.
- Highlight key phrases in italics.

Strengthening Exercises

- Edit Vision, Mission and Strategy until they are enduring statements that "resonate"!
- Drop low-priority items... Remember "less can produce more."
- Refine Objectives and Action Plans to be specific, measurable, and define accountability.

Involve Others

- Few people can write a solid plan by themselves; ask others for feedback.
- Ask your reviewers:
    - Is this plan really strategic? Too optimistic? Too pessimistic?
    - Does it include all of the critical initiatives you have been talking about?
    - Is it too risky? Too safe?
    - Does it reflect your best thinking?
    - What have I overlooked? What do you see, that I missed?
- Listen to the feedback, take notes, and ask clarifying questions.
- Revise and update plan for feedback.
- Ask for another round of feedback.
- Most people find it takes at least three drafts to have a solid plan.
- Repeat until you and your reviewers agree it is solid.

Filling in the Gaps

The process of writing a business plan, in some ways, is like writing a term paper on your non-profit. You capture in writing what you know, conduct research to fill in the gaps, interview knowledgeable people, draft your document, ask for feedback, and then complete the final editing.

Your knowledge of your non-profit is significant. Capture your initial thoughts in the first draft, and then begin the process of reflecting on your plan... and involving others. Keep in mind, the process of planning is one of continual reflection and refinement... and in many ways this is more important than the final document.

Most people have more resources instantly available to them than they realize. These resources are very knowledgeable... and frequently free! They know you, your non-profit, the industry, may share the same clients and may buy from the same vendors.

Resources readily available to you include your team, peer managers, senior executives, Board of Directors, Board of Advisors, vendors, foundations, technical assistance providers, bankers, attorneys, CPAs, and other consultants.

Other significant resources are the national associations. They exist to gather and disseminate information about your industry. They follow all of the trends, innovations, opportunities, regulations, etc. Check out their websites, better yet pick up the phone and talk with one of the executives. Get to know the regular contributors.

One of the benefits of The One Page Business Plan is that it can be read in less than five minutes. Share your plan with your resources. Invite their insights and feedback. Your plan will be stronger!

Implementation... Tracking & Measuring the Plan

Implement Your Plan

Many plans fail because they never get implemented! When great ideas sit on the shelf... nothing happens. Put your plan to work. Your plan is your promise! Your funders and the recipients of your services are counting on the benefits of this plan!

Monitor & Measure

Create a Performance Scorecard for each Objective. Remember – Objectives, if well written, must have a numeric value that is graphable. Included in the Non-Profit Tool Kit CD is a fun and easy template for creating Scorecards. You can graph your results against the Budget or Goal, Last Year and Forecast (if appropriate)... you will have a visual picture of all the key metrics in your organization. It is very simple and easy to determine if your are ahead of target... or behind.

Monthly Business Review

Recent surveys indicate only 1 in 5 organizations have a regularly scheduled monthly review meeting to monitor the implementation and execution of their plans.

The monthly review is a fabulous opportunity to learn what really happened in your organization each month. Do a quick review of each of the major projects... are they on track? If not, address the issues and define solutions to get them back on track.

Have a business coach, professional advisor, mentor? Make it a practice to schedule an hour with them each month to review your progress against your plan.

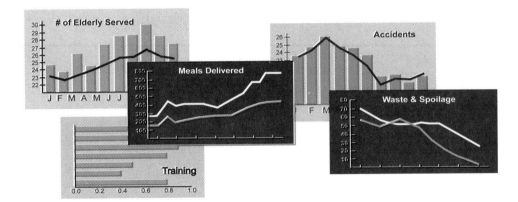

Resources, Timelines and Budgets

Having a plan is critical to your success. Here are a few thoughts on other important processes that will help assure your success.

Define the Required Resources

Every project, program and initiative in your plan will need resources... or it will not happen. For each project identify the people, expense, capital budgets and any other resources required to fully execute the plan. The process of identifying the resources may cause you to realize you may not have the capability or capacity of implementing the plan you just wrote. If that is the case... go back and revise the plan.

Project Timelines

Re-review your project start and completion dates. Are they realistic? One of the major problems with all planning processes is the tendency to think we can do more than we actually can. When we complete a major project or initiative... we feel smart! When we have a list of projects that we have not started or are half done... we feel defeated. Take another hard look at your projects for this next year... would you be extraordinarily pleased if you completed just one or two of them? If so, adjust your plan.

Alignment with Partners & Team

If you have partners or a team, it is not unusual to find during the alignment process that the business units within your organization contributing to projects and programs will not have consistent and appropriate start and completion times. For each major project or program, create an overall timeline to assure all of the sub-tasks are in alignment with the overall milestones. If project dates get changed... be sure to update the plans accordingly.

Create a Budget

Almost every activity in an organization has a stream of revenue or expenses associated with it. Use your One Page Business Plan(s) to help identify all of the sources of revenue, expense and capital. If you need help in budgeting, get it. This is an important part of your success. Included in the Non-Profit Tool Kit CD is a simple One Page Budget Worksheet that should be helpful.

Recommendation: If a business unit, department, project or program is big enough for a One Page Business Plan, it probably should have a separate budget.

■ VISION
■ MISSION
■ OBJECTIVES
■ STRATEGIES
■ ACTION PLANS

Sample Plans...

For some, the easiest way to learn how to write a plan is to take a look at how others have written their plans. In this section we provide thirteen, complete One Page Business Plans for your review. As you can see, the process works incredibly well over a wide variety of social and community services agencies, associations and foundations.

- Oklahoma Jazz Hall of Fame
- Unity in Marin, Spiritual Center
- Burlingame Library Foundation
- Center on Juvenile & Criminal Justice
- Alzheimer's Care Clinic
- Meals on Wheels
- The Wellspring
- Shea Therapeutic Equestrian Center
- Just Say Yes - Educational Technology Foundation
- Pageville Volunteer Fire Department
- Bay Area Entrepreneur Association
- Health Care Foundation - Personnel Manager
- Management Development Program
- Pacific Center

As you review these plans, you will note that they all follow the One Page Methodology fairly closely... but not necessarily precisely. That's OK! Each of these plans is a real plan, written by an executive director, board member, department or program manager... so their personal style comes through!

Note: Sample plans have these consistent characteristics

- <u>Vision Statements</u> paint a <u>graphical picture of what is being built</u>.
- <u>Mission Statements</u> are short, most are <u>8 words or less</u>.
- <u>Objectives</u> are always <u>graphable</u>!
- <u>Strategies</u> describe <u>how</u> the <u>non-profit</u>, department, project or program <u>will be built</u>.
- <u>Action Plans</u> describe the <u>work to be done</u>... <u>all have completion dates</u>.

Oklahoma Jazz Hall of Fame

Chuck Cissel, Executive Director

FY2006 Plan

vision

Within the next three years, grow the Oklahoma Jazz Hall of Fame into an international art institution with annual funding of $1.3 million, providing preservation, education and performance of jazz to music lovers.

mission

Creating Unity Through Music

objectives

- Increase Revenue from $434,947 to $500,000.
- Increase Surplus from $44,878 to $55,000.
- Increase membership from 400 to 600.
- Increase performances revenue from $77,000 to $123,000.
- Increase donations from $374,884 to $750,000.
- Increase grants from $259,784 to $520,000.
- Increase educational program from 3 to 5 & scholarships from four to eight.
- Increase staff from 2 to 6.
- Increase volunteers from 15 to 50.

strategies

- Increase revenues and surplus by promoting performances, galas & space rental.
- Build/attract membership base by promotion, advertising & organization.
- Increase performance rev. by offering diverse programming, increasing frequency & mktg.
- Build donations by dev a capital campaign plan, hiring a dev consultant and a grant writer.
- Engage and educate youth by use of library, computers & practices.
- Expand scholarship endowment by corporate & individual donations & grants.
- Improve Board eff. by targeted recruiting, pre-evaluation & involvement through planning.
- Hire world-class staff by developing specific job descs, for key staff, recruiting and selection.
- Attract/retain volunteer base by membership, marketing & external programs.

action plans

- CC-Complete HR systems job descriptions by 02/28.
- JH-Establish scholarship selection committee by 3/31.
- HS-Roll out volunteer/membership committee by 3/31.
- JJ-Report on Board membership committee by 3/31.
- JH-Dev education committee w/staff member in charge of educational programs by 3/31.
- LS- Dev feasibility study by 5/31.
- CC-Recruit & hire additional staff by 07/31.
- CC-Implement the financial plan to achieve revenue & surplus by 09/30.

Unity in Marin, Spiritual Center

Reverend Richard Mantei

FY2006 Consolidated Plan

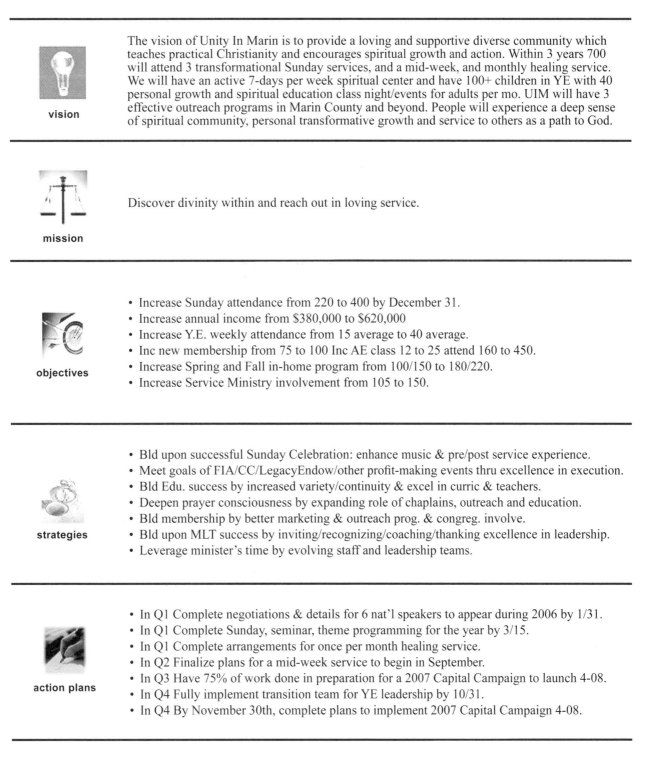

vision

The vision of Unity In Marin is to provide a loving and supportive diverse community which teaches practical Christianity and encourages spiritual growth and action. Within 3 years 700 will attend 3 transformational Sunday services, and a mid-week, and monthly healing service. We will have an active 7-days per week spiritual center and have 100+ children in YE with 40 personal growth and spiritual education class night/events for adults per mo. UIM will have 3 effective outreach programs in Marin County and beyond. People will experience a deep sense of spiritual community, personal transformative growth and service to others as a path to God.

mission

Discover divinity within and reach out in loving service.

objectives

- Increase Sunday attendance from 220 to 400 by December 31.
- Increase annual income from $380,000 to $620,000
- Increase Y.E. weekly attendance from 15 average to 40 average.
- Inc new membership from 75 to 100 Inc AE class 12 to 25 attend 160 to 450.
- Increase Spring and Fall in-home program from 100/150 to 180/220.
- Increase Service Ministry involvement from 105 to 150.

strategies

- Bld upon successful Sunday Celebration: enhance music & pre/post service experience.
- Meet goals of FIA/CC/LegacyEndow/other profit-making events thru excellence in execution.
- Bld Edu. success by increased variety/continuity & excel in curric & teachers.
- Deepen prayer consciousness by expanding role of chaplains, outreach and education.
- Bld membership by better marketing & outreach prog. & congreg. involve.
- Bld upon MLT success by inviting/recognizing/coaching/thanking excellence in leadership.
- Leverage minister's time by evolving staff and leadership teams.

action plans

- In Q1 Complete negotiations & details for 6 nat'l speakers to appear during 2006 by 1/31.
- In Q1 Complete Sunday, seminar, theme programming for the year by 3/15.
- In Q1 Complete arrangements for once per month healing service.
- In Q2 Finalize plans for a mid-week service to begin in September.
- In Q3 Have 75% of work done in preparation for a 2007 Capital Campaign to launch 4-08.
- In Q4 Fully implement transition team for YE leadership by 10/31.
- In Q4 By November 30th, complete plans to implement 2007 Capital Campaign 4-08.

Burlingame Library Foundation

Stephen Hamilton, President

FY2006 Plan (draft)

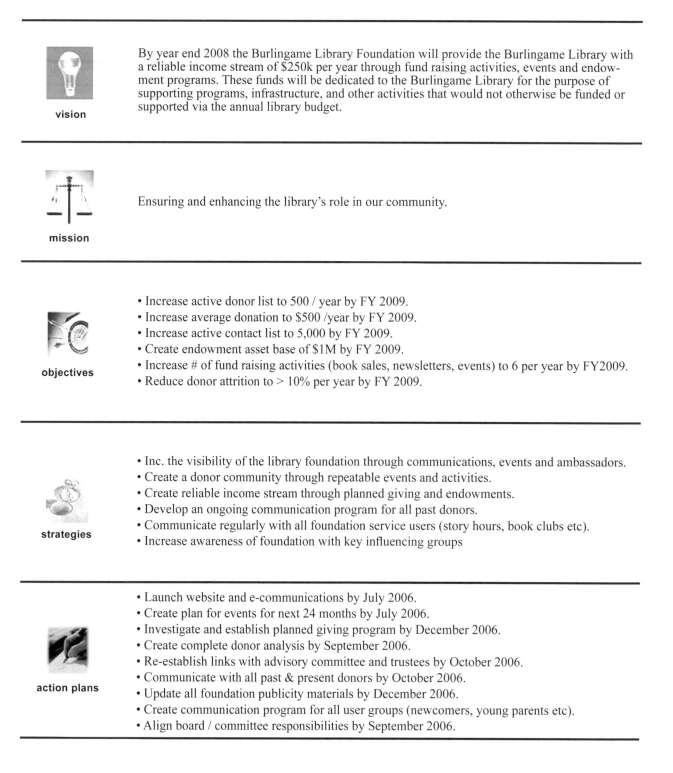

vision

By year end 2008 the Burlingame Library Foundation will provide the Burlingame Library with a reliable income stream of $250k per year through fund raising activities, events and endowment programs. These funds will be dedicated to the Burlingame Library for the purpose of supporting programs, infrastructure, and other activities that would not otherwise be funded or supported via the annual library budget.

mission

Ensuring and enhancing the library's role in our community.

objectives

- Increase active donor list to 500 / year by FY 2009.
- Increase average donation to $500 /year by FY 2009.
- Increase active contact list to 5,000 by FY 2009.
- Create endowment asset base of $1M by FY 2009.
- Increase # of fund raising activities (book sales, newsletters, events) to 6 per year by FY2009.
- Reduce donor attrition to > 10% per year by FY 2009.

strategies

- Inc. the visibility of the library foundation through communications, events and ambassadors.
- Create a donor community through repeatable events and activities.
- Create reliable income stream through planned giving and endowments.
- Develop an ongoing communication program for all past donors.
- Communicate regularly with all foundation service users (story hours, book clubs etc).
- Increase awareness of foundation with key influencing groups

action plans

- Launch website and e-communications by July 2006.
- Create plan for events for next 24 months by July 2006.
- Investigate and establish planned giving program by December 2006.
- Create complete donor analysis by September 2006.
- Re-establish links with advisory committee and trustees by October 2006.
- Communicate with all past & present donors by October 2006.
- Update all foundation publicity materials by December 2006.
- Create communication program for all user groups (newcomers, young parents etc).
- Align board / committee responsibilities by September 2006.

Center on Juvenile & Criminal Justice

Dan Macallair, Executive Director

FY2004-2006 Business Recovery Program

vision

To become the leading organization in the nation on alternatives to incarceration and criminal justice reform by:
- Developing high quality innovative program models.
- Conducting and disseminating high-level policy analysis and research.
- Providing technical assistance to government and nonprofit agencies.
- Developing comprehensive public education strategies.
- Establishing a network of affiliated agencies.

mission

To reduce society's use of incarceration as a solution to social problems.

objectives

- Raise a minimum of $50,000 for new initiatives by July 2005.
- Host two conferences in Sept 2005, funded by foundations to generate $50,000.
- Establish a minimum cash reserve of $30,000 by September 2005.
- Cut monthly operating expenses by $10,000 per month by June 2006.
- Increase agency revenue by 15% in 2005/6 fiscal year from $2.0 to $2.3 million.
- Reduce CJCJ's long-term liabilities by 50% from $500,000 to $250,000 by June 2006.
- Add one new long-term sustainable program generating $250k a year by Sept. 2006.
- Establish a line of credit between $50,000 and $100,000 by December 31, 2006.

strategies

- Immediately reduce all unnecessary expenses, establish frugal mind-set.
- Critically review all staffing positions; selectively eliminate; stay lean.
- Establish much tighter control of contracts, invoicing and collections.
- Negotiate advances on existing and new contracts by asking for more money up front.
- Upgrade accounting staff and systems with assistance of non-profit accounting experts.
- Leverage Board member relationships to negotiate settlements of long term liabilities.
- Expand outreach to long term funders, develop new initiatives to increase revenue.
- Increase individual donor base w/ solicitation letters; use donor list from friends & allies.
- Ensure sustainability by improved program effectiveness & more fee for service work.

action plans

- Complete create overall business recovery plan w/ Board by December 31 2004.
- Initiate fund raising outreach to foundations by July 2004.
- Complete process evaluations for all direct service programs by June 2005.
- Complete internal audit by July 2005 to determine expense reduction opportunities.
- Engage Briones International to manage accounting systems crisis starting 7/1/2005.
- Negotiate with nonprofit loan agencies to establish line of credit by Sept. 2005.
- Fully implement a new accounting system by July 2006.
- Rebuild website to facilitate online fund raising; complete design 11/06; install 01/07.

Alzheimer's Care Clinic

Kim Newton, Executive Director

FY2006 Business Plan Summary

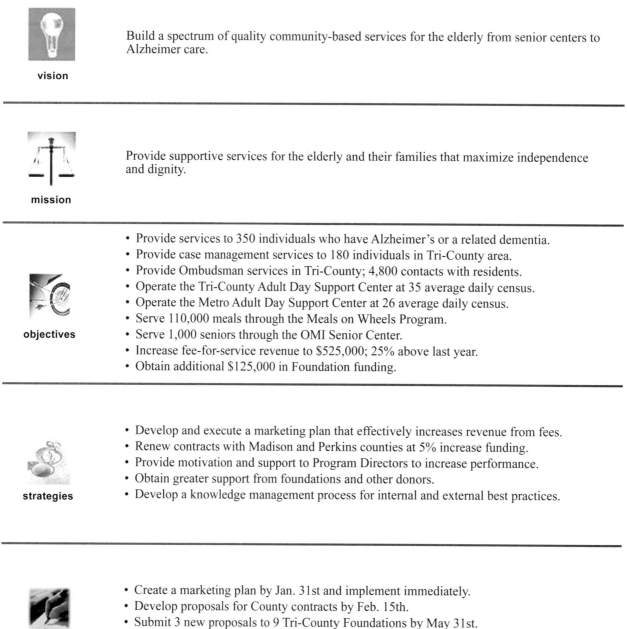

vision

Build a spectrum of quality community-based services for the elderly from senior centers to Alzheimer care.

mission

Provide supportive services for the elderly and their families that maximize independence and dignity.

objectives

- Provide services to 350 individuals who have Alzheimer's or a related dementia.
- Provide case management services to 180 individuals in Tri-County area.
- Provide Ombudsman services in Tri-County; 4,800 contacts with residents.
- Operate the Tri-County Adult Day Support Center at 35 average daily census.
- Operate the Metro Adult Day Support Center at 26 average daily census.
- Serve 110,000 meals through the Meals on Wheels Program.
- Serve 1,000 seniors through the OMI Senior Center.
- Increase fee-for-service revenue to $525,000; 25% above last year.
- Obtain additional $125,000 in Foundation funding.

strategies

- Develop and execute a marketing plan that effectively increases revenue from fees.
- Renew contracts with Madison and Perkins counties at 5% increase funding.
- Provide motivation and support to Program Directors to increase performance.
- Obtain greater support from foundations and other donors.
- Develop a knowledge management process for internal and external best practices.

action plans

- Create a marketing plan by Jan. 31st and implement immediately.
- Develop proposals for County contracts by Feb. 15th.
- Submit 3 new proposals to 9 Tri-County Foundations by May 31st.
- Develop and implement a staff motivation plan by Aug. 31st, includes bonus & prof. dev.
- Meet with key funders at least once every 6 months; first meeting Sept. 20th.

Meals on Wheels

Donna Van Sant, Executive Director

FY2006 Business Plan Summary

ONE
PAGE
PLAN

---

vision

Grow Meals On Wheels program into a premier nutrition service for the home bound elderly and disabled adults in our county, providing a full compliment of quality prepared meals and personal attention seven days a week.

---

mission

At home and healthy with full nutrition and personal attention.

---

objectives

- Provide services to 475 home bound elderly each month.
- Provide expanded nutritional service products to 300 individuals.
- Add new customers at the rate of 45 per month.
- Increase case management revenue to an average of $2,500 per month.
- Recruit and train 25 new route drivers, both volunteer and paid.
- Obtain $80,000 in county contract and foundation funding.
- Provide 12 in-service training sessions for route drivers and 24 for MoW staff.
- Provide nutrition services to 75 disabled adults each month.

---

strategies

- Develop and maintain effective relations with funders; program tours, and proposal writing.
- In conjunction with food services vendors, develop three new products for our customers.
- Develop and execute a customer focused marketing plan for nutrition and CS management.
- Create and execute a staff and volunteer development plan that works!
- Operate our customer feedback and quality control system to increase customer satisfaction.

---

action plans

- Complete new product development by March 23rd.
- Complete staff hiring and support plan by May 16th.
- Hold program tour and meeting with all current funders by October 10th.
- Win funding from 10 new foundations by November 23rd.
- Develop a marketing plan by December 1st.

The Wellspring

Judy Bell, CEO

FY2006 Plan

ONE
PAGE
PLAN

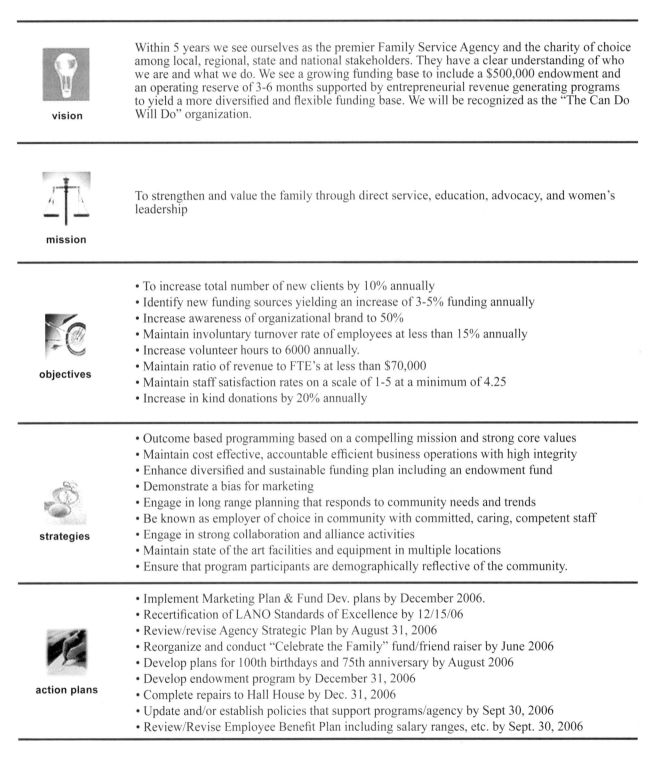

vision

Within 5 years we see ourselves as the premier Family Service Agency and the charity of choice among local, regional, state and national stakeholders. They have a clear understanding of who we are and what we do. We see a growing funding base to include a $500,000 endowment and an operating reserve of 3-6 months supported by entrepreneurial revenue generating programs to yield a more diversified and flexible funding base. We will be recognized as the "The Can Do Will Do" organization.

mission

To strengthen and value the family through direct service, education, advocacy, and women's leadership

objectives

- To increase total number of new clients by 10% annually
- Identify new funding sources yielding an increase of 3-5% funding annually
- Increase awareness of organizational brand to 50%
- Maintain involuntary turnover rate of employees at less than 15% annually
- Increase volunteer hours to 6000 annually.
- Maintain ratio of revenue to FTE's at less than $70,000
- Maintain staff satisfaction rates on a scale of 1-5 at a minimum of 4.25
- Increase in kind donations by 20% annually

strategies

- Outcome based programming based on a compelling mission and strong core values
- Maintain cost effective, accountable efficient business operations with high integrity
- Enhance diversified and sustainable funding plan including an endowment fund
- Demonstrate a bias for marketing
- Engage in long range planning that responds to community needs and trends
- Be known as employer of choice in community with committed, caring, competent staff
- Engage in strong collaboration and alliance activities
- Maintain state of the art facilities and equipment in multiple locations
- Ensure that program participants are demographically reflective of the community.

action plans

- Implement Marketing Plan & Fund Dev. plans by December 2006.
- Recertification of LANO Standards of Excellence by 12/15/06
- Review/revise Agency Strategic Plan by August 31, 2006
- Reorganize and conduct "Celebrate the Family" fund/friend raiser by June 2006
- Develop plans for 100th birthdays and 75th anniversary by August 2006
- Develop endowment program by December 31, 2006
- Complete repairs to Hall House by Dec. 31, 2006
- Update and/or establish policies that support programs/agency by Sept 30, 2006
- Review/Revise Employee Benefit Plan including salary ranges, etc. by Sept. 30, 2006

Shea Therapeutic Equestrian Center

Dana Butler-Moburg, Executive Director

FY2006 Plan

ONE
PAGE
PLAN

---

vision

With the next three years, grow the Shea Center into a preeminent $2 million organization providing therapeutic equestrian activities to a diverse community of people with special needs, and providing internationally recognized education to therapeutic equestrian professionals.

---

mission

Improving the lives of people with disabilities through therapeutic horse-related programs.

---

objectives

- Expand operating campaign to $1.7 Million.
- Raise $1.5 Million through capital campaign.
- Increase annual fund to $250,000.
- Implement bi-lingual programming with 12 families.
- Increase community awareness by 50%.
- Raise $500,000 by June 30 through Campaign Committee leadership.

---

strategies

- Core services include therapeutic riding, hippotherapy, and non-mounted activities.
- Raise capital funds using new campaign committee.
- Redesign and staff annual fund and face-face giving program.
- Increase public awareness through community speaking and media relations.
- Develop campaign prospects through new Board connections.
- Maintain development focus thru weekly review mtgs.
- Develop more effective budget, cost control, reporting systems.
- Dana to be more involved in developing prospects, solicitation and stewardship.

---

action plans

- Hire new business manager to take on operational responsibilities.
- Recreate Campaign Committee by June 30.
- Recruit 5 Comm members (8/31), ID prospect list (9/30), develop new materials (9/30)
- Develop community speaking program (6/30). Deliver monthly talks in Fall.
- Staff Board, all Committees (6/30). Board Training (Sept)
- Begin monthly development meetings (6/15); bi-weekly (9/15).
- Track all objectives through monthly report (6/15)
- Complete equestrian facility (7/31), offices (11/30).

Just Say Yes - Educational Technology Foundation

Robert Chew, Executive Director

FY2000 Plan

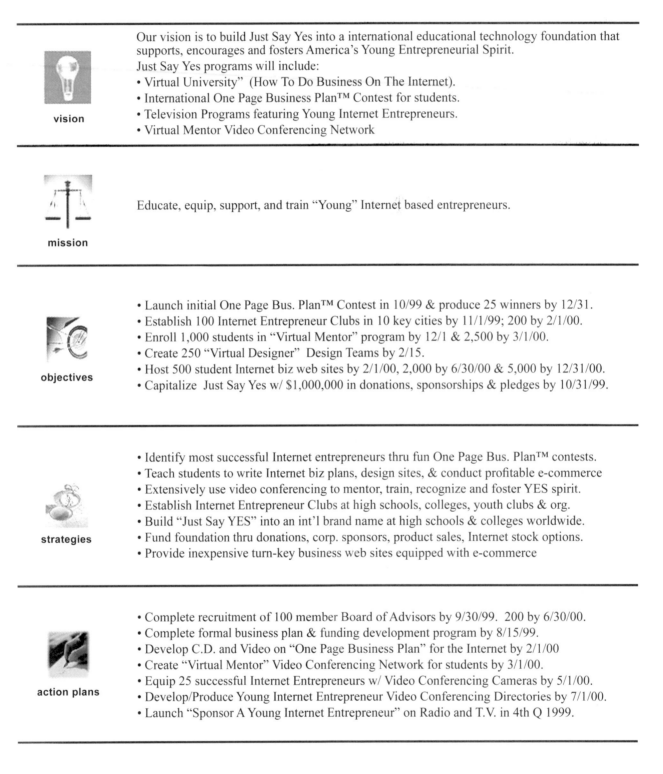

vision

Our vision is to build Just Say Yes into a international educational technology foundation that supports, encourages and fosters America's Young Entrepreneurial Spirit.
Just Say Yes programs will include:
- Virtual University" (How To Do Business On The Internet).
- International One Page Business Plan™ Contest for students.
- Television Programs featuring Young Internet Entrepreneurs.
- Virtual Mentor Video Conferencing Network

mission

Educate, equip, support, and train "Young" Internet based entrepreneurs.

objectives

- Launch initial One Page Bus. Plan™ Contest in 10/99 & produce 25 winners by 12/31.
- Establish 100 Internet Entrepreneur Clubs in 10 key cities by 11/1/99; 200 by 2/1/00.
- Enroll 1,000 students in "Virtual Mentor" program by 12/1 & 2,500 by 3/1/00.
- Create 250 "Virtual Designer" Design Teams by 2/15.
- Host 500 student Internet biz web sites by 2/1/00, 2,000 by 6/30/00 & 5,000 by 12/31/00.
- Capitalize Just Say Yes w/ $1,000,000 in donations, sponsorships & pledges by 10/31/99.

strategies

- Identify most successful Internet entrepreneurs thru fun One Page Bus. Plan™ contests.
- Teach students to write Internet biz plans, design sites, & conduct profitable e-commerce
- Extensively use video conferencing to mentor, train, recognize and foster YES spirit.
- Establish Internet Entrepreneur Clubs at high schools, colleges, youth clubs & org.
- Build "Just Say YES" into an int'l brand name at high schools & colleges worldwide.
- Fund foundation thru donations, corp. sponsors, product sales, Internet stock options.
- Provide inexpensive turn-key business web sites equipped with e-commerce

action plans

- Complete recruitment of 100 member Board of Advisors by 9/30/99. 200 by 6/30/00.
- Complete formal business plan & funding development program by 8/15/99.
- Develop C.D. and Video on "One Page Business Plan" for the Internet by 2/1/00
- Create "Virtual Mentor" Video Conferencing Network for students by 3/1/00.
- Equip 25 successful Internet Entrepreneurs w/ Video Conferencing Cameras by 5/1/00.
- Develop/Produce Young Internet Entrepreneur Video Conferencing Directories by 7/1/00.
- Launch "Sponsor A Young Internet Entrepreneur" on Radio and T.V. in 4th Q 1999.

Pageville Volunteer Fire Department

Robert Lewellyn, Fire Chief

FY2006 Consolidated Plan

ONE
PAGE
PLAN

vision

Within the next three years achieve a fire and emergency services team in the City of Pageville that is characterized by high employee morale and excellent community service.

mission

Elevate citizen confidence that their fire and emergency services are dependable and affordable. Protecting community with quality life… and fire safety services.

objectives

- Reduce fire response time to 5 minutes average by 12/31.
- Reduce freeway emergency response time to 7 minutes average by 12/31.
- Reduce loss of property by 12% from previous year.
- Assure there is no more than a 5% deviation from last year's monthly overtime budget.
- Reduce worker injuries to no more than 6 per month by 12/31.
- 60% employees involved in participation activities by 7/01.

strategies

- Involve community in neighborhood targeted life and safety program.
- Involve all personnel in every aspect of life and fire safety at their locations.
- Establish and enforce performance based accountability system at all department levels.
- Establish and provide professional growth and opportunity programs for all personnel.
- Coordinate with other agencies to meet emergency response standards.
- Deliver safety education & other services within our mission to the community.
- Aggressively work to prevent hazardous conditions.
- Respond promptly to rescues, fires, medical emergencies and natural disasters.
- Ensure safe, professional, environmentally harmonious actions.

action plans

- Develop a coordinating mechanism to keep track of all elements of the strategic plan by 3/31.
- Accountability systems are developed for all elements of the strategic plan by 6/1.
- Implementation of the strategic plan is monitored on a monthly basis by 7/31.
- Develop a list of comparable cities and fire departments to benchmark our services by 9/1.
- A commitment plan to guide building of a policy maker consensus on service levels by 10/1.
- Implement a comprehensive employee involvement plan by 10/31.
- Implement a comprehensive community involvement plan by 12/31.

Bay Area Entrepreneur Association

George Cole, Executive Director

FY2000-2004 Strategic Plan

ONE
PAGE
PLAN

---

vision

Build BAEA into a nationally recognized micro-enterprise organization with an extensive greater San Francisco Bay Area network of entrepreneurial support groups providing nationally recognized products, programs and services to entrepreneurs, small business owners, and partner organizations.

---

mission

Create viable businesses and successful entrepreneurial leaders through networking, support and connection to resources.

---

objectives

- Increase membership from 150 to 300 by December 31st.
- Launch 2 networks by 6/2001 and add 3 more networks by 6/2003.
- Generate $8,000 from entrepreneurial programs, events and products in FY 2000.
- Host 3 regional network events with at least 50 attendees each and generate $3,000.
- Conduct 4 workshops/programs with an average of 25 participants and generate $4,000.
- Increase low-income members to 25 and increase minority members 25% by 3/2001.
- Award 5 scholarships totaling $1,300 in FY 2000.
- Recognize 10 entrepreneurs for outstanding business growth & community service.

---

strategies

- Use public relations and media to share successes, educate, recruit and fund.
- Market and sell BAEA endorsed products and services nationally.
- Collaborate with nat'l micro-enterprise org. in nat'l awareness programs and funding.
- Establish BAEA center to create long-term community presence & financial asset base.
- Enlist key community leaders and businesses to launch and develop new networks.
- Attract/retain low-income entrepreneurs by offering scholarships funded by corp. sponsors.
- Utilize multi-lingual/cultural programs to attract minority entrepreneurs.
- Package successful BAEA programs & products to sell to other micro-enterprise orgs.
- Use technology to manage growth, streamline ops., and deliver programs, & sell products.

---

action plans

- Complete 5-year Strategic Plan by April 30th.
- Complete funding plan by June 15th. Raise $100,000 by November 30th.
- Hire executive director by December 31st.
- Expand board of directors from 4 to 7 by January 31, 2001.
- Develop BAEA product and service marketing plan by March 31, 2001.
- Develop 2-year network expansion plan by June 30, 2001.
- Launch sales/marketing plan of One Page Business Plan by June 30, 2001.
- Collect and write 20 success stories by 7/2001; Implement PR Plan by 8/2001.

Health Care Foundation – Personnel Manager

Jonee Grassi, Personnel Manager

FY2006 Plan

vision

Develop a world class workforce of employees for the Health Care Foundation and their independent contractors who fuel the growth of the organization and its good work through their creativity, dedication, and capabilities

mission

Attract, build and retain a world-class team.

objectives

- Recruit 10 new employees by EOY; end year with 125 employees.
- Decrease turnover rate from 18% to less than 10%.
- Decrease overtime from 22% to 10%.
- Increase average learning program hours/employee to 30 per year.
- Achieve internal promotion rate of 60%.
- Increase flex-scheduling optimization to 90%.

strategies

- Hire world-class team players with exceptional skill sets whenever possible.
- Retain our employees by treating them as strategic partners critical to our success.
- Commit to have resources, people & systems in place before they are needed.
- Ensure career development through innovative training & development programs.
- Fairly compensate employees for their contribution; generous use of flexible benefits.
- Support work-life balance through flex scheduling and well-being programs.

action plans

- Implement Employee Hiring Campaign by 01/15.
- Launch Employee Distance Learning Program by 02/01.
- Develop Intranet Flexible Scheduling facility by 04/15; implement in Q3.
- Complete national salary survey by 06/30.
- Upgrade non-degreed manager development program by 09/30.
- Implement professional skills development program by 11/30.

Management Development Program

Jerome Johnson, CEO

FY2006 Plan

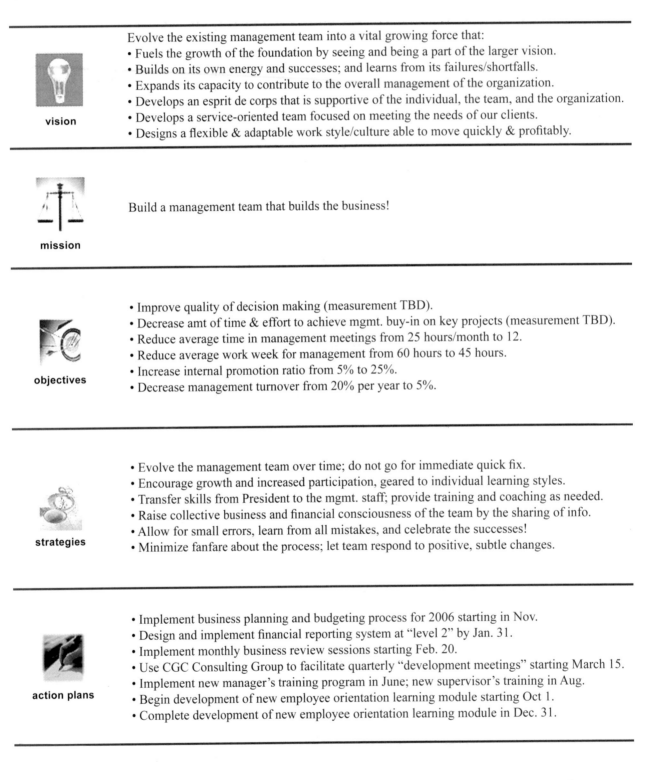

vision

Evolve the existing management team into a vital growing force that:
• Fuels the growth of the foundation by seeing and being a part of the larger vision.
• Builds on its own energy and successes; and learns from its failures/shortfalls.
• Expands its capacity to contribute to the overall management of the organization.
• Develops an esprit de corps that is supportive of the individual, the team, and the organization.
• Develops a service-oriented team focused on meeting the needs of our clients.
• Designs a flexible & adaptable work style/culture able to move quickly & profitably.

mission

Build a management team that builds the business!

objectives

• Improve quality of decision making (measurement TBD).
• Decrease amt of time & effort to achieve mgmt. buy-in on key projects (measurement TBD).
• Reduce average time in management meetings from 25 hours/month to 12.
• Reduce average work week for management from 60 hours to 45 hours.
• Increase internal promotion ratio from 5% to 25%.
• Decrease management turnover from 20% per year to 5%.

strategies

• Evolve the management team over time; do not go for immediate quick fix.
• Encourage growth and increased participation, geared to individual learning styles.
• Transfer skills from President to the mgmt. staff; provide training and coaching as needed.
• Raise collective business and financial consciousness of the team by the sharing of info.
• Allow for small errors, learn from all mistakes, and celebrate the successes!
• Minimize fanfare about the process; let team respond to positive, subtle changes.

action plans

• Implement business planning and budgeting process for 2006 starting in Nov.
• Design and implement financial reporting system at "level 2" by Jan. 31.
• Implement monthly business review sessions starting Feb. 20.
• Use CGC Consulting Group to facilitate quarterly "development meetings" starting March 15.
• Implement new manager's training program in June; new supervisor's training in Aug.
• Begin development of new employee orientation learning module starting Oct 1.
• Complete development of new employee orientation learning module in Dec. 31.

Pacific Center

Juan Barajas, Executive Director

FY2007 Plan

ONE
PAGE
PLAN

---

vision

Within 3 years, grow Pacific Center into a $650,000 sustainable non-profit organization offering a wide variety of human services to the East Bay LGBT community while providing strong leadership and becoming visible as THE community and media voice so all LGBT people ultimately have a place at the table.

---

mission

Connecting the LGBT Community in the East Bay!

---

objectives

- Secure $139,500 in foundation grants by 4/1/07.
- Earn $90,000 in clinic revenues by 6/30/07.
- Raise $67,500 in individual donations by 6/30/07.
- Reduce overhead costs by 10%, from $81,000 to $73,000 by 6/30/07.
- Increase # of POC clients from 40% to 50% by 6/30/07.
- Increase # of transgender clients from 10% to 15% by 6/30/07.
- Increase# of senior clients from 10% to 15% by 6/30/07.

---

strategies

- Become the leading voice & media resource of the SF East Bay LGBT community.
- Create a culture of creativity, forward-motion, and partnership with all stakeholders.
- Grow Pacific Center w/ a fundraising board, increasing PR, & developing new programs.
- Dev. strong relationships w/ key leaders thru mtgs., attending commty events, & networking.
- Inc. client diversity thru outreach to target groups, improved language capacity, & staff trng.
- Improve svcs. thru program integration, offsite delivery, & effective client feedback system.
- Strengthen clinic through more eff. screening, improve client tracking, & intern supervision.
- Connect w/ media by regular press releases, dev reporter relationships, & ptnr w/ GLAAD.
- Increase staff capacity through new intern positions, volunteer recruitment, & mgt training.

---

action plans

- Attract & place new program, development, and communications interns by 10/1/06.
- Implement donor acquisition, cultivation, & appreciation program by 10/1/06.
- Initiate organizational creativity & collaboration culture shift by 10/1/06.
- Fully implement diversity outreach and service capability by 11/1/06.
- Complete overhead reduction project by 2/1/07.
- Roll out service improvement project with 1 new offsite service location by 2/15/07.
- Secure one new STRATEGIC service, advocacy, overhead reduction partnership by 3/1/07.
- Complete board recruitment by 4/1/07.
- Run 3 Bay Area media stories by 5/1/07.

Acknowledgements

This book could not have been created without the incredible work of hundreds of our dedicated One Page consultants who helped thousands of non-profit executive directors, their Boards and their staffs craft their One Page Business Plans over the last seven years. To them I express a deep heart felt thanks!

To list all of the people who contributed in little and big ways to taking a simple concept, a one-page plan, and adapting it to the world of non-profits would take multiple pages. However I wanted to personally express my gratitude to the individuals listed below for their creative ideas and suggestions on how to make The One Page Business Plan a truly effective tool for non-profit organizations. Their creative input and suggestions were significant to the initial design of this book; their feedback on the final manuscript was invaluable! I thank you!

Ed Allen	Amy Grossman	Pete Meldrum
Linda Andersen	Peter Hackbert	Bonnie Meyer
Alan Aurich	Bob Haddad, Jr.	Gary Montrezza
Hoyit Bacon	Catherine Hambley	Toni Nell
Kevin Bartram	Stephen Hamilton	Jerry Pinney
Leyna Bernstein	John Hansen	Nika Quirk
Larry Boone	Brent Henley	Dr. Ruth Ramsey
David Bracker	Arnie Hendricks	Jena Rhea
John Brown	Ray Hilbert	Cynthia Riggs
Ray Brun	Mike Holmes	Chuck Ruebling
Dick Buxtson	Jerome Johnson	Diane Ruebling
Bob Chew	Madeline Kellner	Bill Seelig
Brenda Chaddock	Bob Kramer	John Seidel
Wayne Chittenden	Pete Krammer	Bud Seith
Lynn Ciocca	Greg Krauska	Jessica Siegel
George Cutler	Daniel Lieberman	Dennis Smith
Douglas Diamond	Chuck Longanecker	Ann Squires
Bill Drennan	Dr. Denise Lucy	Tracy Tamura
Joy Duling	Dan Macallair	Skip Torresson
Bob Dupriest	Richard Mantei	Mike Verhey
Ronn Ellis	Maria Marsala	John Weld
Kent Ellsworth	Catherine Marshall	Mary Ann Wetzork
Jerry Fletcher	Karen Mathre	Terry van der Werf
Chuck Fry	Heidi Maye	Ron Wilder
Bob Garrett	Dean McCormick	Kara Witalis
Don Goewey	Harvey Meier	Roger Witalis

If You Liked this Book... You Will Love These Special Versions!

For the Professional Consultant
If you are a proprietor of know-how this book was written for you! You get proven templates and examples on CD that reflect best practices. Easy assessments let you quickly discover what's working in your practice and what's not!

For the Financial Professional
If you are in insurance, investments or related industries this book is what you need to move ahead now! Proven templates and examples in the book and on CD reflect best practices. Assessments let you easily discover what's working for you and what's not!

For Non-Profit Organizations
Thousands of non-profits have already successfully written and implemented One Page Plans. This special version helps directors, boards and volunteers clearly define and live up to their promises. Includes desktop planning CD and organizational assessments.

For the Creative Entrepreneur
This is the million-dollar seller that forever changed the way people write and implement business plans. For startups and well established companies both large and small. Includes desktop planning CD along with easy to do business assessments.

Final Thought...

 Most of us have no shortage of good ideas! The issue is which ideas are we going to act on?

Learn how to say no to "good ideas"... yours, your managers, employees, associates, friends and family. You only have time, money and resources to execute against the "great ideas." The great ideas can be written on the back of an envelope. They are memorable! They catalyze people and organizations.

Planning doesn't need to be complex! Keep it simple!

Jim Horan
President
The One Page Business Plan Company

The One Page Business Plan Company

Workshops and TeleClasses

The One Page Business Plan® is available to your non-profit or organization as a workshop, annual retreat, teleclass or complete planning program. Experienced facilitators will tailor the presentation to meet your needs.

All classes and programs are hands-on working sessions designed to teach participants how to write a clear, concise, understandable business plan, on a single page, in the quickest and simplest way possible.

Enterprise Planning Software

This innovative system uniquely links The One Page Business Plan with an Executive Dashboard and a Simplified Project Tracking System that can be used in small service agencies, foundations, hospitals, churches, associations, and large global non-profits.

The system requires no IT support and can be learned in 30 minutes. Interested? The One Page Planning and Performance System is rapidly becoming the planning system of choice for executive directors and CEOs of non-profits.

Professional Certification

We are interested in partnering with experienced business, government, and not-for-profit consultants and coaches. If your firm provides strategic planning and/or performance management consulting services, The One Page Business Plan may be a profitable addition to your toolkit.

Coaches and consultants who successfully complete the training and certification programs will be licensed to market and deliver One Page Business Plan products and services.

The One Page Business
Plan Company
1798 Fifth Street
Berkeley, CA 94710
Phone: (510) 705-8400
Fax: (510) 705-8403
jhoran@onepagebusinessplan.com
www.onepagebusinessplan.com

Non-Profit Tool Kit
How to Install and Use the CD

Installation Instructions:
Simply load the CD into your CD drive. requires Microsoft Word® and/or Excel® to use the templates, forms and spreadsheets. Open any Directory with a double-click. Select desired Word® document or Excel® spreadsheet.

CAUTION:
Immediately after opening any of the files we encourage you to save the file with a new name using the "SAVE AS" command in order to preserve the original content of the file.

No Technical Support
This CD is provided without technical or software support. Please refer to your Microsoft Word® or Excel® User Manuals for questions related to the use of these software programs.

System Requirements:
Windows 95/98/NT/2000/XP
Macintosh OS 9.1 or higher
Microsoft Word® and Excel®
CD/ROM drive